Jewish Woman in Jewish Law

THE LIBRARY OF JEWISH LAW AND ETHICS
VOLUME VI

EDITED BY NORMAN LAMM

President and Jakob and Erna Michael professor of Jewish philosophy
Yeshiva University

Jewish Woman in Jewish Law

by

Moshe Meiselman

KTAV PUBLISHING HOUSE, Inc./New York

YESHIVA UNIVERSITY PRESS/New York

1978

Library of Congress Cataloging in Publication Data

Meiselman, Moshe
Jewish woman in Jewish law.

(Library of Jewish law and ethics; 6)
Includes bibliographical references and index.
1. Women—Legal status, laws, etc. (Jewish law)
2. Women, Jewish—Religious life. I. Title.
Law 296.1'8 77-5100
ISBN 0-87068-392-2

MANUFACTURED IN THE UNITED STATES OF AMERICA

Contents

Acknowledgments

The author and publisher thank the following for permission to reprint:

Philip Feldheim Inc. for sections from *The Psalms: Translation and Commentary by Rabbi Samson Raphael Hirsch* © 1960 Philip Feldheim Inc. and *The Hirsch Siddur* © 1972 Feldheim Publishers.

Judaica Press Ltd. for sections from *The Pentateuch Translated and Explained by Samson Raphael Hirsch* © 1971 The Judaica Press.

West Publishing Co. for sections from Thomas E. Atkinson, *Wills* © 1953 West Publishing Co.

Editor's Foreword

The feminist movement of recent years has, inevitably, turned its attention to the Jewish tradition. The critique of Judaism—specifically, of the role of Jewish women in Jewish law—has frequently been more hysterical than historical, more apoplectic than apodictic. The millennial Jewish concern for the protection of woman's welfare and dignity in a world where these were not at all taken for granted, was simply ignored or, worse, stood on its head. Nothing that the Jewish tradition had to say about women, it seemed, could be right. If a statement was openly misogynistic, it was taken to be characteristic of all Jews at all times. If it was clearly in favor of women, it was accused of being patronizing and condescending. Thus, advocates of the Jewish tradition were caught in a "double bind," and there was no opening for rational discourse and analysis.

Not all the criticism, of course, was part of this feminist frenzy. Some of the liberationist animadversions were measured and thoughtful. Even those who struck out wildly at almost every Jewish position were usually motivated by genuine concern and perplexity.

The action elicited an equivalent reaction. Defenders of the tradition either shouted back, matching decibel for decibel, or acted as if there was nothing to discuss. Whatever, the rhetoric was more notable for its temperature than for its luminosity.

The present volume by Dr. Moshe Meiselman is, to my knowledge, the first full treatment of the subject by a staunch advocate of the Jewish tradition, presented in a manner both thoughtful and scholarly. One need not agree with every position taken by the author to be grateful to him for his reasoned analysis and for the multitude of sources he has gathered to support his interpretations. But it is not agreement with his position that is important, as much as the opportunity to hear the quiet and reasoned analysis of a young Jewish scholar who knows his material, who has engaged the contemporary issues with respect and sympathy, and who asks only that we pause long enough to turn the debate into a dialogue.

The concerned layman and the scholar alike are surely indebted to Dr. Meiselman for this contribution.

NORMAN LAMM

August 5, 1976

Preface

The purpose of this work is to evaluate the issue of feminism from a Jewish perspective. Such an effort requires a study of certain fundamental areas of Jewish thought. The feminist critique of Judaism, as in fact much of contemporary life, is based on a very definite value structure which is at odds with Jewish values on a number of basic points. The book, therefore, begins with an introduction to the Jewish value system. This is followed by a brief analysis of the story of creation. In Jewish thought, the story of creation is not merely of historical interest. Its prime significance is that it puts into perspective certain essential aspects of the human personality. Therefore, an analysis of the creation of woman becomes important for any study of the position of woman in Jewish thought. Because the Bible views marriage and family as essential elements of the divine plan of creation, my treatment of these topics follows the discussion of creation. I then proceed to evaluate the position of women in Jewish law.

The range of topics required to evaluate properly the topic of the Jewish woman in Jewish law would fill many volumes. In any limited work, such as this one, the author must select the areas most germane to the interests of his audience. I have selected my topics with an eye to the current feminist critique of Judaism. Hence, some topics were omitted and others treated lightly.

This volume is an outgrowth of a series of lectures given by me at the Hillel Foundation of Northwestern University. The arranging of those lectures, and whatever success they enjoyed, is due in large part to the efforts and kindnesses of Rabbi Mark Gellman and Mr. Murray Goldenhersh. To them I give my thanks.

The distance between the spoken word and the written word is justifiably long. When one attempts to make the transition, he should recall the famous dictum of the Beth Halevi: "Not all that is thought should be said, and not all that is said should be written, and not all that is written should be published, and not all that is published should be read." The spoken word allows the lecturer the luxury of question and defense, of reinterpretation and recall, none of which is granted the author. Thus, the demands of excellence which fall upon a writer far exceed those encountered by the lecturer. Furthermore, the spoken word is oriented to a specific audience; the written word, to everyone.

Nevertheless, this trepidation may be carried too far. Sometimes issues present themselves which must be addressed in print. To allow oneself the luxury of years of research and writing, even when wise from a scholarly point of view, might be foolish from a practical perspective. Practical considerations demand early responses to current issues. It is in this spirit that I present this volume.

Many people have helped me prepare the manuscript for publication. In particular, I would like to mention Rabbi David Bleich, Professor Dale Gottlieb, Professor Jacob Landynski, and Professor Alan Lazaroff, who all gave so readily of their time and learning. Their comments, efforts, and friendship are deeply appreciated. I would also like to thank Rabbi Norman Lamm, the editor of this series, for his many helpful comments and suggestions.

In order to maintain a historical perspective, I have indicated the approximate date of death of all post-talmudic scholars quoted in the body of the text. In addition, I have added some brief explanatory material about the major works in the bibliography. For the reader who wishes a more detailed introduction to rabbinic literature, chapter 1 of David Feldman's *Birth Control in Jewish Law* is highly recommended.

Some of the material treated required a familiarity with

details of the Anglo-American legal tradition, and to acquire this I have consulted with a number of legal scholars. In addition, the kindness and courtesy of the library staff of Northwestern University Law School have enabled me to research the material as thoroughly as possible.

Translations from the Hebrew are generally my own. Transliteration has generally followed the rules set down by the *Jewish Encyclopedia.* I have deviated from this system in two instances. The transliterations *beth-din* and *tzitzit* are so commonly used that to transliterate as *beit-din* and *ẓiẓit* would be confusing.

Finally, *aḥaronah aḥaronah ḥavivah,* my deepest gratitude must be expressed to my wife, Rivka Leah, whose encouragement and support were indispensable in the preparation of this book. Many of the major ideas expressed in the book were inspired by her comments, but more importantly by her example.

חלקי ה׳ אמרה נפשי על כן אוחיל בה׳
טוב ה׳ לקוו לנפש תדרשנו

Chicago, Illinois
25 Adar I 5736

כ״ה אדר ראשון תשל״ו

Introduction

The contemporary observant Jew is caught in a vicious trap. On the one hand, he is bound by Jewish tradition, which touches his life at every moment and in every sphere. On the other hand, he has been raised and educated in a society whose goals and values are often in conflict with the actions prescribed or proscribed by his tradition.

To escape this trap, he must choose one of three courses. The first is to become an "observant Jewish secularist," that is, to adopt the goals and values of the secular environment and to use the Jewish tradition to determine one's day-to-day actions. This course, followed by many, is really no escape at all. Not only does it precipitate personal conflicts that can never be resolved, but on a more profound level, it makes Judaism nothing but shallow formalism. God does not merely demand the allegiance of our hands and feet, although these too are of paramount importance, He demands the entire individual, and the observant Jewish secularist fails to render unto God what rightfully belongs to Him: the human personality. In contemplating the observant Jewish secularist, I am often reminded of the prophet Isaiah's condemnation of those who offer God but the most empty of formal oblations: "Why do I need the multitude of your offerings, says the Lord, . . . Who has required this of you, to trample my courts?" (Isa. 1:11–12).

A second alternative for the contemporary observant Jew is to retreat into simple piety and not address himself to outside issues. This approach too leaves much to be desired, although simple piety, for all its lack of sophistication, does have deep religious significance and in many respects constitutes a valid approach to life for the average man.

The ideal solution—and like all ideals it is too seldom realized—is to integrate the goals and values of the Torah into one's personality and to acquire them as his own. Only in this manner is a human being able to serve God totally and to render unto God what is truly His.

Part I

The Question of Perspective

When presenting the topic of woman in Jewish law to a general audience, one must first introduce the value structure of Judaism—the perspective from which a Jew views life. To study Jewish law from an alien point of view would be to strip it of its vital source. This is an immediate consequence of the fact that Judaism is not just a series of legal dicta, but a comprehensive, self-justifying and self-defining value system. Hence, for an honest understanding of any segment of the legal data of Judaism, the law must be viewed from within the structure of Jewish values.

We must therefore be careful to avoid the twin temptations of apologetics and "disinterested" scholarship. The apologist tries to show the consistency of Judaism with another value structure, generally that of his audience—"You are liberal, Judaism is more so; you are conservative, Judaism is more so; you like ecology, Judaism likes it better." The apologist's characteristic approach—"Anything you can do, Judaism can do better"—never works because it is essentially dishonest. Judaism fits into its own value structure and into no other.

The disinterested scholar presents the legal material objectively and allows his audience to evaluate it from within their own value structure. This approach does not suffer from the dishonesty of apologetics, but it is also insufficient, because the general audience is not shown the value structure within which the legal material is meant to be viewed.

Therefore, no attempt will be made here to demonstrate the consistency of Judaism with the moral-axiological views of contemporary America. This work, rather, will treat the topic of woman from what is, in the author's opinion, the perspective of Jewish values. As a brief introduction to feminism and Jewish law, I will outline the basics of Judaism so that the reader will be able to evaluate the law from within its native structure.

1

The Source of Jewish Values

The story of creation, as viewed by Jewish tradition, establishes God not only as the One who brought the physical universe into being, but also as the source of moral law. The Midrash tells us that the moral and physical worlds are not independent of each other.[1] God created the physical universe with a moral purpose. Just as a builder does not build randomly, but proceeds from a prearranged plan to achieve his desired end, so God had a plan when He created the physical universe. Our tradition teaches that the moral principles of the Torah were the prearranged plan which determined the patterns of physical creation. The laws of the Torah, tradition continues, preceded physical creation. To realize the moral end of creation, man was fashioned to serve as that being who would bring moral order into the universe. There is, hence, no contradiction between the laws of the Torah and human nature. The God of nature and the God of the Torah are one.[2]

However, the relationship between the physical and moral laws is of a more profound nature. For the Jew, the very notion of a creation ex nihilo carries with it an inescapable conclusion. That is to say, the creation of the universe includes the creation of the rules which govern the universe. The physical and moral rules that govern the world are not a priori. Both were brought into existence by God Himself, both represent His will, and neither is justified by anything other than His will. The fundamental laws of gravity, for instance, are themselves a creation. In the words of the Psalmist: "*He* has given a law [i.e., the laws of nature] which shall not be transgressed" (Ps. 148:5).

The fact that the divine will, which is self-justifying, lies at the base of all physical law, is implicit in the nature of scientific investigation. When a scientist asks the question "why?," he is doing one of two things. Either he is looking for the principle underlying a specific phenomenon or he is taking a specific principle and looking for an even more basic principle. When Newton saw the apple drop and asked "why?," he was looking for the underlying principle of which the falling apple was a specific application. His quest, of course, ended with the discovery of the laws of universal gravitation. When a contemporary physicist contemplates the laws of gravity and asks "why?," he is searching for an even more fundamental law. However, the physical world offers no answers to the ultimate why, since physical laws, ultimately, are merely an expression of the divine will.[3]

This reasoning applies not only to the physical world but to the moral world as well. Creation ex nihilo implies to the Jew that everything is derived, finally, from the divine will. The moral law, like the physical, is a result of the self-justifying divine will. Physical creation occurred subsequent to the establishment of the moral code and was accomplished in conformity with its goals and principles.

While the divine will is sufficient in the area of physical law, the establishing of the moral code is more complex. Physical law is forced upon us by God. Creation, by definition, establishes God as the source of physical law, but we are given freedom in moral decisions.

In the moral sphere, God is the source of ethics for three reasons. First and most basic, because God is omnipotent and has prescribed serious punishment for those who transgress His will and bountiful reward for those who fulfill it. To the imperatives "Thou shalt" and "Thou shalt not," weak, finite, earth-ridden man can only submit in dutiful obedience. Indeed, for many people reward and punishment provide the sole motivation for adhering to the moral law.

However, the tradition has always spoken disparagingly of

those who do not move beyond this stage to higher levels of service.[4] The tradition makes no distinction among those who utilize the Torah for their own ends—whether financial reward, ego satisfaction, or spiritual reward. God must be served and His will followed for the intrinsic value of God's word.

The compelling nature of God's word is derived from the two concepts of *yirat ha-romemut* and *ahavat ha-shem*. Man's awareness of God's overwhelming otherness, of His infinite wisdom and power, and of his own limited and finite nature, lies at the basis of the proper attitude toward God. This awe of transcendence—*yirat ha-romemut*—itself compels obedience and submission to the divine will. However, Judaism proceeds beyond *yirat ha-romemut* to *ahavat ha-shem*, love of God. The basic concept which underlies *ahavat ha-shem* is the experience of God as the ultimate source of all value and worth—as He who is valuable beyond all conceiving. These two concepts—*yirat ha-romemut*, awe of transcendence, and *ahavat ha-shem*, love of God—which arises out of the experience of God as absolute value—establish the basis of the moral law.

The Shema, the fundamental statement of Jewish belief, expresses this idea clearly. It begins with the statement, "Hear [more accurately, "Understand"], O Israel, the Lord is our God, the Lord is [the only] one" (Deut. 6:2). The statement of unity is interpreted by the Talmud[5] and Midrash[6] as referring to God's total uniqueness and otherness. This uniqueness and otherness provide the basis for *yirat ha-romemut*, awe of transcendence. The Shema then proceeds to the love of God: "And thou shalt love the Lord thy God with all thy heart and with all thy soul and with all thy might." It is only from this point that the subsequent verses can and do proceed to discuss the moral law.[7]

The fundamental place in religious morality occupied by the perception of God as the source of absolute value was also recognized by the famous German theologian, Rudolf Otto, who wrote:

> It is not that the awe of holiness is itself simply "fear" in face of what is absolutely overpowering, before which there is no alternative to blind awe-struck obedience. "You alone are holy" is rather a paean of praise which so far from being a faltering confession of the divine supremacy, recognizes and extols a value, precious beyond all conceiving. The object of such praise is not simply absolute might making its claims and compelling their fulfillment, but a might that has at the same time the supremest right to make the highest claim to service and receives praise because it is in an absolute sense worthy to be praised.[8]

The distance between man and God is not only in might, or in wisdom, but also in value. God is ultimate value, and man's life acquires value only through his relationship with God. This concept lends true ultimacy to the religious moral life. Man achieves value in his life only by surrendering his independent claims to value and realizing his unique and special relationship to the source of all value.

Judaism categorically rejects Kant's use of man's reason as the source of ethics. Kant regarded man's rationality, and that alone, as the source of ethics, but to Judaism man cannot be the source of ultimate value. Man acquires ultimate value only because on the sixth day of creation he was created in the image of God. The Midrash elaborates upon this theme by declaring that man was created in the image of a monkey as well as in the image of God, and thus if man were to reject his godly image, he would be left with nothing but the image of a monkey.[9]

Judaism also unequivocally rejects the basic axiom of humanistic and much liberal thinking that man per se is the source of value. We read in Leviticus: "If anyone sins and rebels against the Lord and deals falsely with his neighbor . . . " (Lev. 5:21). The Tosefta comments on the order of the phrases in this verse: "No man deals falsely with his neighbor unless he first rebels against God."[10] Since belief in God is the basis of all morality, the rejection of morality is ultimately based on the rejection of God.

The Talmud sees a similar idea in the order of the Ten Commandments.[11] The first commandment is: "I am the Lord, your God" (Exod. 20:2). This provides a basis for the subsequent universal commands of human morality. Man himself cannot be the source of morality.

Every ethical system addresses itself, explicitly or implicitly, to the question of the source of value. Any compelling ethical motivation, even in the area of interhuman relations, is built on the assumption that human life possesses some intrinsic value; Judaism sees this value exclusively in man's relationship to God. Schweitzer found the source of value in the concept of life, others found it in the human being himself, still others in the concept of human society, but Judaism found it in God. Since God is the sole source of value, He is the sole arbiter of moral action.

The fundamental statement of Jewish monotheism, "Hear, O Israel, the Lord is our God, the Lord is [the only] one" (Deut. 6:2), is much more than a rejection of polytheism or of a trinitarian understanding of God. It affirms that no power in the world, physical or moral, coexists with God. Thus, there can be no axiological absolutization of anything but God Himself. To set up man, the state, or any concept as a moral absolute is a total violation of the command "the Lord is [the only] one."

Thus, in the realm of the moral law also, the question "why?," is not the essential question. Since the essence of moral imperative is the divine will, with its own intrinsic justification, beyond that there is no why. The moral why, like the physical why, is nothing but a search for the underlying principles of divine will. He who is the source of our physical reality is the source of our sense of value.

The physical-divine will followed the moral-divine will chronologically. The physical world came into being as the place where the moral divine will would be realized. Physical creation was not accomplished in an amoral context but rather in the context of the moral divine will. Physical creation had a direction and a moral purpose; that is why the Midrash declares that creation found its fulfillment in the revelation at Sinai.[12]

It will be useful to summarize our discussion at this point. The Jew's motivation for serving God is threefold. At its simplest, it is merely fear of retribution and anticipation of reward. The next level is an awed awareness of God's overwhelming otherness. The highest level is the realization and acceptance of God as the ultimate source of all value and worth, i.e., love of God. The Talmud ascribes the steps from the first and second levels to the third to Abraham.[13] It points out that he was the first person to understand that God is to be worshipped not only as the supreme power, the unification of the entire pagan pantheon into one being, but also as an *adon*, or master, who has the ultimate right to make demands of man. That is why Abraham is held up as the exemplar of love of God.

2

Creation of Woman

In Genesis we read of the dual quality of the creation of man. As a purely physical being, man was created from the dust, as were all the other animals. But man was elevated above the other animals and endowed at creation with a divine spark. This divine essence, referred to by the Bible as *ẓelem elokim,*[1] man's divine image, or *nishmat ruaḥ ḥayim,*[2] the breath of the spirit of life, defines man's spiritual nature and gives ultimate value to his life.

The creation of woman also reflects the duality of human existence. The Bible records together the creation of woman and the creation of man in the image of God: "And God created man [the human being] in His image, in the image of God did He create him [the human being], male and female He created them" (Gen. 1:27). A distinction is drawn, though, with regard to the physical creation of woman. She was not created from dust, as was man and as were all the other animals, but rather from the body of man. The reason for this, we shall see, was to establish the proper framework for marriage.

The Talmud gives us a second interpretation of the sequence of verses relating to the creation of woman.[3] It suggests that the first person was a self-sufficient androgynous being. Thus, the verse in Genesis tells us: "Male and female He created them," i.e., the first human being was both male and female. God, however, said that it is not good for a human being to be totally self-sufficient and devoted only to himself, and therefore He divided this person into two separate human beings, one male and one female, each with his own individual talents and personality. Either one, alone, is incomplete. The completion and perfection of the human personality occurs when man and woman live for each other, give to each other, and function together as one unit, each performing his and her own unique tasks.

In explaining the nature of creation, the Raavad comments:

> It is for this reason that God saw fit to change the order of creation when He came to man. For had He created man and woman from the earth, each independently, each would have gone his own way. Husband and wife would not be designated one for the other to live together, for they would have been created separately. Rather, God created woman from man so that they should live together as one unit, each one needing the other.[4]

Marriage is man's natural state. All human beings are necessarily incomplete without a mate, and it is through marriage that completion is achieved. Marriage and family are integral parts of the divine plan. They are not arbitrary and unnatural institutions created by society, but rather reflect an important aspect of human nature. The biblical verse describing marriage, "Therefore shall a man leave his father and his mother and cleave unto his wife and they shall be one flesh" (Gen. 2:24), follows immediately upon the creation of Eve. It is a natural consequence of the manner of creation.

The Raavad continues that the manner of creation not only makes marriage the natural state of man, but also defines the proper relationship within marriage. The basic attitude of marital partners to each other must be one of *ḥesed*. *Ḥesed* is that character trait which Judaism felt must underlie all interpersonal relationships. It is the basis of all Jewish ethics. *Ḥesed* is the ability to give to another out of a sense of closeness and identification with that other's needs. One who gives out of *ḥesed* does so because the other's need is as real to him as his own. The story of creation, the Raavad continues, tells man that the ideal marriage is the one in which he treats his wife as he would himself, because, in a very real sense, she is a part of him.[5] Hence, Jewish law requires a man to be as concerned about his wife as he would be about himself. The marriage relationship is the paradigm of *hesed*, for in marriage one is continually required to focus on another and to be as sensitive to the other's needs as one would be to one's own.

The Bible's role definition for woman follows upon the story of creation: "And Adam called his wife Eve, for she was the mother of all life" (Gen. 3:20). In the Bible, the assigning of a name is not only the giving of an arbitrary title but is also an essential part of role definition. To give Eve the name "mother of all life" is to assign her that task as her fundamental, though not necessarily exclusive, role.*

The Midrash states that this role definition results from the nature of creation.[6] Implicit in woman's creation was a command that she develop a specific trait of the human personality to its maximum—the capacity for *tzniut*.[7]

The root צנע, *ẓena*, occurs twice in the Bible, once in the verse ואת צנועים חכמה *ve'et ẓnuim ḥokmah* "Those who are *private* [in their Torah learning] will achieve wisdom" (Prov. 11:2), and once in the verse, "He has told you, man, what is good and what the Lord demands from you, but to do justice, love kindness, and to walk *privately* with your God" (Mic. 6:8). When anyone, male or female, serves God, he must concentrate on the inner dimensions of his personality. *Tzniut* is

*It should be observed that man's naming of woman in Genesis 2:23 and later in Genesis 3:20, is unlike his naming of the beasts. Whereas man's imposition of names upon the beasts asserts his cognitive superiority and physical mastery over them, in Eve's case his name acknowledges God's will acting independently of and prior to his own. The assignment of the name *ishah* in Genesis 2:23 is subsequent to God's statement in Genesis 2:20. The name Eve is given only after God has given a second role assignment in Genesis 3:16, as a result of the initial sin of Adam and Eve. This point is overlooked by Mary Daley in *Beyond God the Father*, Boston, Beacon Press, 1973.

the inner-directed aspect of striving, the essence of the Jewish heroic act. Woman was enjoined to develop this trait of personality to its highest degree. This is symbolized by the fact that woman was created from a part of the body which is private in two senses—first, it is generally clothed, and second, it is located beneath the skin.

But in the Jewish context, hidden from public view does not imply inferiority. For instance, in Genesis, when the angels visit Abraham, they ask him: "Where is Sarah, your wife?" Abraham answers: "In the tent" (Gen. 18:9), to which Rashi cites the comment of the rabbis: צנועה היא, *znuah hee*, "Sarah is a private person." Yet we find that Sarah achieved greater spiritual stature than Abraham. A few chapters later we read that God instructed Abraham: "All that Sarah tells you, hearken to her voice" (Gen. 21:12), to which Rashi comments: "This teaches us that Sarah was superior to Abraham in prophecy." Although in their life together Abraham took the public role, this implies absolutely nothing about personal importance or spiritual greatness, for the Jewish hero is the hero of the inner stage, not the public stage.

Tzniut is not restricted to women. The high points in the lives of the major male figures of the Bible occurred in private. This is made most explicit in the story of Jacob's fight with the angel.

> *And Jacob was left by himself* and a man fought with him until dawn. And he saw that he could not defeat him and he smote him on his hip. And Jacob's hip was dislodged while fighting with him. And he [the man] said: "Send me, for the dawn is rising," and he [Jacob] said: "I will not send you unless you bless me. . . ." And he said: "No longer shall you be called Jacob, but Israel, for you have fought with God and with men and have emerged victorious." [Gen. 32:25–29]

The last verse is very puzzling. What does it mean to fight with God? Onkelos offers a different translation: "For you have fought before God and against men." The name Israel, according to his translation, indicates before whom one acts and to which audience one attaches significance. It tells us that Jacob's struggles were performed only for the sake of God and not for the sake of any human audience.

This idea is implicit throughout the Bible. When Abraham and Isaac reached the high point of their moral lives in the episode of the Akedah, they did so in front of no audience but the Almighty Himself. They had been accompanied on their journey by Ishmael and Eliezer, but upon approaching the mountain, Abraham told his servants: "You stay here . . . the lad and I must go on . . . " (Gen. 22:8).

When Joseph withstood the temptations of Potiphar's wife, the high point of his moral life, we read: "And no member of the household was there in the house" (Gen. 39:11). When the high priest, on Yom Kippur, entered the Holy of Holies, we read: "And no man may be in the Tent of Assembly from when he comes to atone in the Holy Place until he leaves" (Lev. 16:17).

How different they are from Greek heroes! Perhaps the clearest example is the contrast between the Akedah and the Greek tragedy *Iphigenia in Aulis.* While Abraham sacrificed Isaac to God, for God, and before God alone, Agamemnon sacrificed Iphegenia for Greece and in the presence of Greece. The essence of the Greek heroic act lay in its public appeal and public nature. There was no glorification of inner heroism, but only of public display and public approval.

Far from the shores of Aulis was the Jewish hero. To the Jew, moral victory for both man and woman is what one does for God and before God, the source of all value. Jewish tradition frowns upon public display, for the moment a human acts in public, his motivation can be tainted by unworthy considerations.

> R. Yoḥanan said: "A covenant has been drawn up that he who toils in his Torah study in private does not quickly forget, as it says: 'And those who are private will achieve wisdom' [Prov. 11:2]."[8]

An important aspect of the religious-moral act is its privacy, far from the approval of the crowd. It is in this light that we understand the classic Jewish legend that the world is maintained in each generation through the merit of thirty-six hidden saintly persons. The highest achievement is that of the hidden saintly man who toils his whole life for God's approval alone.

Thus, the verse כל כבודה בת המלך פנימה, *kol kebudah bat hamelekh penimah,* "The entire glory of the daughter of the king lies on the inside" (Ps. 45:14), is absolutely nonpejorative. This verse, which underlies much of the Jewish attitude toward the female role, has been used in rabbinic literature in two ways. First, it has been viewed as a statement of the private nature of the female role,[9] and second, as a panegyric on the private nature of the religious experience in general.[10] The Midrash unifies the two interpretations and sees the same underlying thread running through both applications of the verse—true achievement is always in the private sphere, hidden from the public eye.

> "And God spoke to Moses in the Wilderness of Sinai." [Num. 1:1] Before the Tent of Assembly was erected, He spoke to him from the bush . . . and afterwards in the land of Egypt . . . and afterwards in Midian . . . and afterwards at Sinai . . . but after the Tent was erected He said: "How beautiful is *tzniut* [privacy]!" as it says: "And to walk privately with your God" [Mic. 6:8], and therefore He spoke with him in the Tent. And so too did David say: "The entire glory of the daughter of the king lies on the inside, more so than the one who is clothed in golden garments" [Ps. 45:14].* The daughter of the king is Moses, who is the king of Torah. The one clothed in gold is Aaron [this refers to the eight golden garments worn by the high priest]. Hence, it is said that a woman who is private in her

*The King James translation is: "The king's daughter is all glorious within; her clothing is of wrought gold." The translation in the text accords with the midrashic interpretation.

> life [and hence plays Moses' role by emphasizing private religious experience], even if she is an Israelite, is deserving to marry a priest and give birth to high priests.† This is what the Holy One said: "It is my glory to speak on the inside."[11]

Aaron, the high priest, performed his divine service publicly. Moses spoke to God in private and thereby achieved a higher religious level. In the spiritual dimension, public exposure is very often a handicap rather than an asset.

Public and private are necessary aspects of the lives of both men and women. Neither sex is restricted to either area, but tradition did say that the private sphere should be the dominant area of a woman's life. However, even a man, whose primary involvement is public, was reminded that his highest achievements are the acts that he does in private.

†This is based on a dual interpretation of the above verse in Psalms. The first one translates the words ממשבצות זהב לבושה *mi'mishbeẓot zahab lebushah* as "more so than he . . ."; the second interprets as saying: "her garments will be the priestly golden garments."

3

Family: The Focus of Jewish Life

The family is the basic unit of society, and if this is true of society at large, it is certainly true in Jewish life. Despite opinions to the contrary, the synagogue is not the focus of Judaism. The center of Jewish life has been, and will always be, the home. The collapse of traditional Judaism in America followed the collapse of the Jewish home, not that of the synagogue. The synagogue broke down in the mid-twentieth century because the traditional family had been secularized several decades earlier. When contemporary critics of Judaism claim that the synagogue is the center of Jewish life, it is because they have tasted only the most insipid and sterile forms of Jewish existence.

The Jewish woman is the creator, molder, and guardian of the Jewish home. The family has always been the unit of Jewish existence, and while the man has always been the family's public representative, the woman has been its soul.

The creation of a Jewish home is no small task. It requires much more than the burdens of childbearing, childrearing, and menial household tasks, for to create a Jewish home is to create a new link in the chain of Jewish existence and tradition. It is not easy to form children in the Jewish mold and prepare them to become Jewish adults, and such a task would not have been primarily assigned to women had they not been especially prepared for it, physically, psychologically, intellectually, and spiritually, by Almighty God Himself. Moreover, the raising of Jewish children cannot be performed simply by a day-care center, for this task requires a unique spiritual being on a high spiritual level. "Hearken my son to the discipline of your father and do not forsake the Torah teachings of your mother" (Prov. 1:8). While a Jew ideally learns Torah discipline primarily from his father, he learns the fundamental concepts and principles of Judaism primarily from his mother. A child needs both parents, each performing a specialized individual role.*

A primary aspect of the mother's role is to communicate the fundamentals of Jewish belief and practice to her children. She must teach her children to know God, love Him, fear Him, and worship Him, and she must bring the concepts of God and His service to life for them. The vibrancy of these concepts gives the Jewish home its unique power, and the subsequent religious life of every Jew is dependent on the success of this early maternal teaching.

There are many facets to homemaking. Providing for the physical needs of the members of the household is only one part of a Jewish housewife's work. While this responsibility is generally a necessary component of her job, her most important task is to provide the religious base for her children and the proper religious environment for all members of the household. In such a context, even the physical aspects of homemaking achieve a spiritual dimension.

Since Jewish tradition viewed the maintenance of home life as critical, both husband and wife were expected to participate in it. Primary responsibility was assigned to the mother, but the father was expected to take, and did take, an active role in the religious upbringing of the children. Judaism has always condemned the absentee father who takes little or no part in the rearing of his children.

The phrase "Jewish home" has suffered much in recent literature. It has been stereotyped and maligned to such a degree that most people are ashamed of the Jewish mother and

*These two tasks mesh together and each partner must participate with the other's work. We are talking only of primary responsibility.

the Jewish home. But the stereotype is false—"Jewish home" does not connote chopped liver and gefilte fish! The Jewish home is a unit of great vitality whose functioning expresses the divine way of life that is the Torah. The principles of the Torah are not mere intellectual abstractions; they must be brought to life in the Jewish home. The Jewish home is the center of our existence; it is the place where sanctity and Torah are translated into real life, where children are imbued with the principles of Judaism and adults live in accordance with the divine will. The Jewish home is not merely for children, but for adults as well. The Talmud tells us not only that the success of R. Yehoshua ben Ḥanania was due to his mother,[1] but also that the success of R. Akiva[2] and the catastrophe of R. Elazar ben Arakh[3] were due to their wives.

The Midrash relates a most indicative and telling tale:

> It is told that a pious man was married to a pious woman and they were childless. They said: "Our life together does not benefit the Almighty One," and they divorced. He married a wicked woman and she made him wicked. She married a wicked man and made him righteous. It follows that all depends on the woman.[4]

On a day-to-day basis, it is the woman who provides the general home atmosphere that will determine her family's spiritual direction, for better or worse.

The Jewish woman is the soul and inspiration of the Jewish home. Through building this home she achieves her ultimate Jewish self-definition, and the stamp she leaves on the home expresses her own uniqueness and individuality.

4

Biblical Women

The Jewish people have always treasured the stories in the Bible, using them as sources of examples to follow in their own lives.[1] Biblical figures have served as role models for countless generations of Jews, both male and female. The biblical heroine is a strong woman totally involved in the building of her home and her people. The role she plays is crucial, and is shown to have a critical influence on the future and nature of the Jewish people.

In the story of Abraham and Sarah, Abraham is obviously the major public figure. Sarah is kept very much in the background. This idea, implicit in the biblical text, is made explicit by the rabbis in their comment that "Sarah was a private person."[2] However, when the proper environment of Abraham's home was threatened by Ishmael's behavior, and the negative influence of Ishmael on Isaac threatened Jewish survival, Sarah acted quickly. While Abraham, who was preoccupied with his public role, lacked the proper insight into the situation, Sarah demanded: "Drive away the maid servant [Hagar] and her son" (Gen. 21:10). The moral implications and the daring of this statement reveal the strong role that Sarah played in Abraham's home. When Abraham hesitated, the Bible tells us, God said to him: "All that Sarah tells you, listen to her voice . . . " (Gen. 21:12). God Himself upheld the morality and correctness of Sarah's demand.

Sarah was not motivated by hatred of Hagar or by jealousy, for if this had been the case, God would not have upheld her. The rabbis tell us that Sarah was upheld because she had achieved a higher level of prophecy than Abraham. Her spiritual insight and sensitivity had shown her the dangers for Isaac created by Ishmael's presence in Abraham's home.[3]

After Sarah passed away, we are told very little about Abraham's activities. Sarah's role could not be taken over by Keturah. The children of Abraham who did not grow up in Sarah's home, under her guidance, did not become his spiritual heirs. Abraham had eight sons. Only Isaac, born of the appropriate mother and educated by her, was fit to carry on Abraham's work.

The life of Rebecca and Isaac is a striking parallel to that of Abraham and Sarah. "And Isaac brought her to the tent of Sarah, his mother" (Gen. 24:67). Rebecca took over Sarah's role. When Isaac lacked the necessary insight to evaluate Esau's true character, Rebecca, acting in a morally courageous manner, preserved the future of the Jewish people. In this instance, Isaac himself recognized the correctness of Rebecca's actions.

The difficulties facing Leah and Rachel were of a different order. The Bible does not say that they performed actions as dramatic as those of Sarah and Rebecca, but they were assigned a more difficult task—that of creating a proper environment for Jacob within the negative atmosphere of Laban's home. The moral difficulties they faced were of a day-to-day nature, but the two women were successful—the twelve sons of Jacob all remained true to the spiritual calling of their fathers, becoming the foundation pillars on which the Jewish nation was built.

This picture of women possessing the moral strength and determination necessary for the formation of the Jewish people is a constant theme throughout the Bible and the rabbinic commentaries to the Bible. For example, at a critical point in Jewish history, it was the moral courage of the midwives that saved the nation.[4] Again, when the Jewish men were overtaken by despair during the period of servitude in Egypt, it was their wives who kept the hope of redemption alive.[5] Similarly, when Amram decried the frustration of bearing children in Egypt, his daughter Miriam prevailed upon him not to destroy the Jewish people out of overreaction to frustration.[6]

Women are constantly presented as figures of great moral strength during periods of crisis. On the fortieth day after Sinai, the male population panicked at Moses' apparent disappearance. The men brought catastrophe upon themselves by making the golden calf. The women, on the other hand, did not panic and refused to participate in the making of the calf.[7] Later, when the spies reported that an attempt to conquer Canaan would result in disaster, the determination of the men collapsed again at a moment of crisis. The rabbis tell us, however, that the faith of the women held strong, and hence the women were not included in the decree sentencing the entire generation of the exodus to die in the wilderness.[8]

The picture of the Jewish woman, held up for future generations, is uniform. It is a picture of moral strength and determination that survives periods of crisis and provides the foundation upon which the Jewish home can be built.

Is it any wonder that the rabbis said: "Each generation is redeemed because of the righteous women of that generation"?[9] The women have given the Jewish people their moral strength, and that strength enabled the Jews of each generation to survive the crises they faced.

5

Marriage: The Ethical Dimension

Must a woman be limited to the home? Is man's role defined in terms of himself and his career, and hence primary, while woman's role is defined in terms of her contributions to others, and hence secondary, as many feminists claim? What role is there in Judaism for the woman who does not want to marry? What role is there for the woman who wishes to pursue a career outside the home?

Marriage is important in Judaism for two basically distinct reasons, one ethical and the other religious. The Torah says: "It is not good that man be alone" (Gen. 2:18). The word *good* is both an ethical and a practical judgment. On the most practical grounds, it is not good for man to remain alone. Man is a social being who craves contact with others,[1] but he also requires marriage for another dimension of his life: his ethical completion.

Hesed is one of the foundation stones of the Jewish personality. It is that attribute of the Almighty to which is appended the adjective *rav,* "great."[2] A Jew, required to follow God's example in the ethical sphere, is required not only to practice *ḥesed* but to do so in abundant measure. Maimonides says:

> There is no greater or more exalted joy than to gladden the heart of the poor and the orphan and the widow and the stranger. The one who gladdens the heart of the downtrodden is compared to the Almighty as it says: "For He revives the spirit of the low ones and the heart of the downtrodden" [Isa. 57:15].[3]

Hesed is more than the formal dispensing of charity. It includes the ability to shift the entire focus of one's concern. It is not performed for the moral pleasure of doing good, but rather because of a total identification with the other's troubles and sorrows.

Many people feel that by concerning themselves with others they are serving their own moral advantage.[4] Since they relate to others in a morally functional manner, they view the recipient of a moral act as the means for their own achievement in the moral sphere. Judaism does not look positively on such charity for it is totally self-centered.[5] *Hesed* is rather a total shift in one's personal concern. A person who acts out of *ḥesed* does not act from concern for his own moral advantage, but from a genuine concern for the other's welfare.

There are, in effect, two distinct mitzvot of charity.[6] The first command requires the giving of money or other material sustenance to the poor. The second is more intangible. It requires the donor to feel the pain of the poor and be concerned with their problem, for the pain of the poor must be as real to him as his own. Someone who sees charity as a means for his own moral advantage cannot experience this emotion because he is still too concerned with himself. *Ḥesed* requires the merging of our own concerns with those of our neighbor, so that we no longer think only in terms of ourselves.

It is for this reason that the *Sifre* says that *ḥesed* begins with those who are closest to us, first with our family, and then with our neighbors. To shift the direction of our concern, it is necessary to begin with those who are closest to us and then to encompass our neighbors and finally the rest of the world.[7]

Marriage is the beginning of *ḥesed*, for in marriage one is obligated to shift the focus of his concern from himself to his wife and children. A person who refuses to marry does not want to shift the focus of his concern to a mate or to children, but wants to live by and for himself. "It is not good for man to live alone" (Gen. 2:18), for to live alone is to deny the foundation of Jewish ethics, the experience and emotion of *ḥesed*.

Hesed is required on all levels of human existence, and it is demanded of both men and women in the performance of their ultimate tasks. The feminist claim that in Judaism men serve themselves, while women must serve others, is totally unfounded. The verse in Proverbs refers to a "Torah of *ḥesed*,"[8] which prompts the Talmud to ask: "Is there a 'Torah of *ḥesed*' and a 'Torah not of *ḥesed*'?"[9] The Talmud answers that he who studies so that others may benefit by his learning is exemplary of the "Torah of *ḥesed*," and he who studies for his own religious edification, with his own religious growth as the central focus of his concern, is exemplary of the "Torah not of *ḥesed*." For the latter person, the Talmud has only scorn.[10]

To say that women are judged religiously by their contributions to the religious achievements of others, and men by their own achievements, is nothing less than a modern-day perversion of the entire message of Judaism. The attitude toward *ḥesed* is the essential difference between oriental and Jewish spirituality. The Eastern mystic concentrates completely on his own spiritual development. Self-involvement is an essential ingredient of Eastern spirituality. But to a Jew—male or female—spirituality and religious fulfillment lie in "service." *Ḥesed* is a major component of the Jewish religious act. There is no greater achievement for a man or woman than an act of *ḥesed*.

The Talmud tells us an important story.[11] Motivated by his idealistic and self-sacrificing wife, R. Akiva became the outstanding Torah scholar of his age. He returned to Jerusalem accompanied by twelve thousand students. As his wife made her way to greet him, he told his students: "All the Torah that you and I have learned we owe to her." Rachel, the wife of R. Akiva, achieved greatness through her contribution to the accomplishments of others. Her greatness came from her selfless pursuit of *ḥesed*. However, this is true not only of Rachel, but also of her husband. The essence of R. Akiva's life was the teaching of Torah, and it was for this that he martyred himself.

He was sentenced to death by the Romans for teaching the Torah. His teaching was an act of *ḥesed*, especially when to do so went against his best personal interests, for a man must study not merely for his own spiritual growth but also to share his knowledge with others. He must be concerned with their spiritual growth as well as with his own.

Both men and women are obligated to pursue *ḥesed* as an essential part of their ultimate tasks. *Ḥesed* may dominate a woman's life, but it is also an important part of a man's life and religious achievements. No one, either male or female, may use the Torah for his own selfish purposes.

6

Marriage: The Religious Dimension

Marriage is important to the Jew on another level as well. The highest ideal to which a human being can aspire is to dedicate his life completely to the service of God. For a woman, this means the creation of a Jewish home. For a man, this generally means a complete and total involvement in the learning of Torah. This obligation, though, is coupled with a second obligation. A man must transmit his learning to his children and to his students.

A striking delineation of these two tasks was given by Rabbi Aaron Soloveichik. Naḥmanides and R. Baḥya ben Asher state that the command of passing the Torah on to the following generation includes passing on the experience of revelation, as symbolized by the fire of Sinai, and the content of revelation, as symbolized by the voice from Sinai.[1] Moses was instructed that when he came to the Jews: "Thus shall you say to the house of Jacob and tell the children of Israel" (Exod. 19:3). The rabbis say that the house of Jacob refers to the women, and the house of Israel to the men. The primary task of the women, according to Rabbi Soloveichik, is to pass on the experience of revelation, while the primary task the men is to pass on the content of the revelation.* The command to the women was given first because handing on the experience of revelation is more important than handing on the content of revelation. R. Baḥya says: "For if one forgets the experience he will end up by denying the content." Without the *mysterium tremendum,*

*These two tasks mesh together and each partner must participate in the other's work. We are talking only of primary responsibility.

Judaism becomes an entirely secular, uninspired experience, with no lasting power.

Those who themselves do not feel the awesome responsibility and importance of the task of communicating the fire of Sinai may see the woman's role as minor and secondary. But for an inspired Jew, who keenly feels the fire of Sinai, the task of transmitting this feeling to future generations is certainly not secondary. It is a task of the utmost importance and responsibility. It is a task which cannot be shirked by anyone within whose heart the fire of Sinai burns brightly.

Just as a man is judged after death essentially in regard to his success in carrying out his ultimate task, so too is a woman judged essentially by her success in her ultimate task. The Talmud describes rewards and punishments for individual moral acts and rewards and punishments for life goals.[2] Needless to say, while the reward for a specific moral act is limited in scope, the reward for achievements in life goals is most extensive. In this area men and women are equally judged and given equal rewards,[3] but for different tasks—man for the creation of a link in the chain of Torah scholars, woman for the creation of a Jewish home.

But here a final word of caution must be injected. With her glorification of the contemplative life, Greece produced a concept of man radically different from the Jewish concept. For the Greek, self-definition was attained through intellectual activity; for the Jew, it is attained through religious performance. Judaism extols the intellectual act not for the Platonic reason that mind is superior to body, but because of the essentially religious nature of the study of the Torah. Divorced of its moral and religious qualities, the intellectual act is intensely selfish,[4] and thus even the study of the Torah as a purely intellectual and nonreligious act is severely condemned.[5] Hence, in lauding intellectual involvement for its essentially religious nature, Judaism equally lauded the creation of a Jewish home for its essentially religious nature. They were lauded equivalently because religiously they are equivalent. Neither can exist without the other, and neither is superior to the other.

In conclusion, we must keep in mind that these functions are not exclusive, but represent initial points of emphasis and primary responsibility. Because of social and economic exigencies, it may be that women had little Torah education in the past, but this represented a specific social situation rather than a norm. On the other hand, except for the most extreme cases, it is unheard of for a Jewish husband not to share with his wife in childrearing. This sphere of the home activity was given such preeminence that both partners had to share in it.

However, there is a critical difference between what is mandated and what is praised as the highest form of life. The degree to which a woman's ultimate task—the building of a Jewish home—is mandatory can best be seen by comparing it with man's requirement to pursue his ultimate task.

While to divorce one's life from all else but the learning of Torah is the highest way of life for a man, it is not obligatory. Two passages from the Talmud express this idea clearly. R. Shimon ben Yoḥai was sentenced to death by the Roman government. He and his son hid in a cave. After twelve years,

> they left the cave and saw a man who was plowing and planting. R. Shimon said: "How do they forsake eternal matters [such as the study of Torah] and engage in temporal matters?" Whatever they looked at was immediately destroyed. A heavenly voice told them: "Have you left the cave to destroy my world? Return to the cave." They returned and sat there for twelve months.[6] . . . Thereafter a heavenly voice said: "Go out of the cave." . . . R. Shimon said to his son: "My son, it is enough for the world to have two people such as you and me totally involved in Torah." That Friday afternoon they saw an old man take two fragrant bunches of myrtle leaves[7] and run home with them. At evening time they asked him: "What are these for?" He answered: "To honor the Sabbath with them." They asked: "Would not one suffice?" He answered: "One to correspond to the command

> *Zakhor* and one to correspond to the command *Shamor.*"[8] R. Shimon said to his son: "See how dear are the mitzvot to the Jewish people! "[9]
>
> Our rabbis taught that the verse "And you should harvest your grain" was written, for it says: "This Torah shall not depart from your mouths and you shall think about it day and night" [Josh. 1:8]. Lest one would take these verses literally, the Torah says: "And you should harvest your grain" [Deut. 11:14[—act in consonance with the ways of the world. These are the words of R. Yishmael. R. Shimon ben Yoḥai said: "Is it possible that a man should plow at the time of plowing and plant at the time of planting and reap and thresh at the proper times? What will be of the Torah?"[10] . . . Abaye said: "Many followed R. Yishmael and were successful; many followed R. Shimon ben Yoḥai and were not successful."[11]

R. Shimon gave three reasons for demanding of everyone a life of complete dedication to religious involvement. First, the command to learn Torah places a demand on all of one's time. The biblical verse says: "And you shall think about it day and night" (Josh. 1:8).

Second, it is essential for Jewish survival that all Jews be totally conversant with the entire tradition. Thus, R. Shimon exclaimed to R. Yishmael: "What will become of Torah?" Third, when one chooses something of transitory value over something of ultimate value, i.e., worldly pursuits over a dedication to Torah, he indicates that he considers the value of Torah secondary to the value of what he has chosen. We are not allowed to assign Torah a secondary position in our lives. To do so would violate the command: "For he has been contemptuous of the word of God" (Num. 15:31).[12] A proper evaluation of the significance of God's Torah would make it impossible to choose any other activity above involvement in Torah. Thus, R. Shimon exclaimed to his son: "How can they forsake something of permanent significance for something of temporary significance?"

R. Shimon subsequently learned the answers to his questions. The Talmud tells us that the command to study Torah must be viewed in the context of an individual's requirement to engage in constructive activity and earn a living. R. Shimon further said to his son: "It is enough for the world if you and I engage in study." The passing of the tradition from generation to generation requires only the intense learning of the highest scholars and teachers. The learning of the masses, he realized, is important, but not essential, for Jewish survival. Finally, R. Shimon commented to his son: "See how dear are mitzvot to the Jewish people." One whose life is permeated with an absolute dedication to mitzvot, but also earns a living, does not thereby necessarily equate the Torah with other activities.

R. Shimon's way of life, total involvement in the Torah to the exclusion of everything else, is certainly the highest ideal to which a Jew can aspire. But it is not designed for everyone. It is only for enlightened individuals who aspire to spiritual greatness. The average man achieves his spirituality through the performance of mitzvot.[13] But the man who aspires to spiritual greatness, while he certainly performs the mitzvot, goes beyond them to total involvement in the study of Torah.

Maimonides formulates this concept in the following manner:

> And why did the tribe of Levi not acquire a portion in the land of Israel or in the booty of the other tribes? It is because they were separated to serve God and teach His just ways and righteous laws, as it says: "They shall teach Your Laws to Jacob and Your Torah to Israel" [Deut. 33:8]. Therefore are they separated from the ways of the world, they do not participate in wars like the rest of Israel, nor do they acquire possessions by physical means, for they are the army of God, as it says: "May God bless His army" [Deut. 33:11], and He will provide for them, as it says: "I am your portion and inheritance" [Num. 18:20]. But this is true not only of the tribe of Levi, but of any and every human being whose spirit has dedicated itself and

> whose mind has understood to separate himself and to stand before God, to serve Him, to know Him, and to walk in paths of uprightness as God has made him. This man, who has removed from his neck the burden of worldly considerations which other men seek out, has sanctified himself in the most holy manner and God will be his portion and inheritance forever and ever, and He shall give to him in this world that which is necessary for him, as He has granted to the priests and the Levites.[14]

The religious ultimate of complete and selfless dedication is open to all, but it is expected only of the tribe of Levi. The man who does not choose this path, and instead follows the path of worldly involvement, has two options. He may choose the path of the tribe of Zebulun, of whom we read: "Rejoice Zebulun in your goings out, and Issachar in your tents" (Deut. 33:18). Rashi comments in the name of the rabbis: "Zebulun and Issachar entered into a partnership between themselves. Zebulun settled on the coast and engaged in commerce and earned money. Issachar sat and toiled in Torah." Zebulun converted his worldly work into a religious dedication by sharing with Issachar the results of his labors, and hence Zebulun's work is considered of a high religious quality, rivaling, according to some, Issachar's labor.[15]

The other option open to the man who chooses to pursue a worldly occupation is to have his work become nothing but a self-serving, self-involving, self-gratifying activity. Any activity whose focal point is service of self cannot be religiously noteworthy. The Torah has allowed us to choose our level of dedication, and he who chooses the minimal path has willingly chosen for himself a religiously minimal life.

The general pattern for women is strikingly similar. As we have seen, woman's ultimate task is to build a Jewish home. While enabling is a fundamental part of both the male and female roles, it dominates and defines the female role. The *Arukh ha-Shulḥan*[16] uses this fact to explain the talmudic statement: "Greater is the reward given to women than the reward given to men."[17] This means that the essential role of women in building the home is similar to the role of Zebulun, whose reward is greater. The Talmud tells us elsewhere that "the enabler of an act is greater than the performer."[18] Enabling is a fundamental Jewish act and not a secondary level of performance.

But a woman, unlike a man, is not required to marry.[19] A woman's decision to marry is totally optional, as is a man's decision to dedicate himself totally to the learning of the Torah. A person's ultimate task is totally optional, and he may choose the level of his service.

For the woman who chooses not to marry, as for the man who chooses to pursue a worldly occupation, two paths are open. Just as the tribe of Zebulun pursued its ultimate task by supporting the efforts of the tribe of Issachar, so a woman may devote herself to the specific tasks of a Jewish woman in a supportive manner. However, if she wishes, she may exercise the option of simply pursuing a career. As with a man, however, any activity whose focal point is merely service of self cannot be religiously noteworthy. The essential idea of *ḥesed* is to place the focus of activity outside oneself. *Ḥesed* is incumbent upon both men and women. It is one of the most essential, if not *the* most essential, traits of character, that Judaism demands of its adherents, both male and female.

While only a minority of Jewish men, through the ages, have selflessly dedicated themselves to complete involvement in Torah, Jewish women have always selflessly dedicated themselves to their ultimate task of building the Jewish family. Jewish women, throughout the ages, have made the proverbial *eshet ḥayil*, "woman of valor," a living reality.[20] It is true that because of economic exigencies most men have not chosen the path of complete involvement in Torah. This consideration has not been present for women as acutely as for men. But this factor alone does not explain everything. The natural maternal instinct of women, which goes back, as we saw earlier, to the divine plan of creation, combined with a great capacity for *ḥesed*, has been an equally important factor. While both men and women are required to practice *ḥesed*, women have far outdistanced men in performing acts of *ḥesed*.[21] Woman's capacity for *ḥesed* has sustained the Jewish people throughout the generations. Jewish survival does not require the entire male populace to be totally involved in the study of Torah, but it does require the dedication of all Jewish women to the task of building Jewish homes. Thus, while women are not required to pursue their ultimate task, women throughout the generations have willingly accepted the burdens of household and childrearing. This selfless act of *ḥesed* has ensured the survival of the Jewish people in each generation.[22]

7

Torah Knowledge for Women

All authorities agree that women are exempt from the obligation to learn Torah.[1] The Mishnah discusses the propriety of teaching Torah to women, but never entertains the idea that they are obligated to study. However, to say that women are not required to involve themselves in Torah study, while certainly true, oversimplifies the situation.

The Mishnah says:

> Ben Azzai said that a man must teach his daughter Torah.... R. Eliezer said that he who teaches his daughter Torah is considered as if he had taught her *tiflut*.[2]

The word *tiflut* has been interpreted in two ways. Most have understood it to mean "trivial and irrelevant things."[3] This interpretation identifies *tiflut* with the root *tofel*, as found in the verse "Can that which is tasteless [*tofel*] be eaten without salt?" (Job 6:6). An alternative interpretation of *tiflut* is "immorality."

Maimonides, who adopts the first interpretation, is most explicit. Certain areas of study are intrinsically esoteric and can be understood, even on a minimal level, by only a very limited group. Torah, Maimonides says, is not so. "It is accessible to all, young and old, man and woman, those with great minds and those with limited ones."[4] Torah may be accessible to all on their own level, but solid accomplishment on any level requires complete dedication of time and effort. Since, as Maimonides says,[5] women are not generally ready to dedicate themselves completely to Torah study,[6] their knowledge will necessarily be superficial. Given such superficial knowledge, a woman will not be able to appreciate the depth and scope of Jewish learning and will come to consider it irrelevant and trivial, i.e., *tiflut.*

The alternative translation of *tiflut* as "immorality" reasons in a similar manner.[7] Superficial knowledge can easily be misdirected. One of the major areas of Halakhah where one relies on a woman's judgment is that of family purity. A woman who has only superficial knowledge in this area may make halakhic decisions that involve both her husband and herself in a violation of these very important laws.

It is true that the rabbis approached the learning of Torah by women with great caution. Superficial knowledge is dangerous in all areas, independently of whether the possessor of the knowledge is male or female, and it is especially dangerous in so crucial and complex an area as Torah. Thus the Talmud asks: "Who is an evil, sly man?"[8] Ulah answered "it is one who studies the Bible and the Mishnah, but has not learned from the wise men." Rashi explains that he who has not learned sufficiently to acquire a deep and thorough understanding of his material and hence will not know how to apply his knowledge in practice. "R. Elazar said that such a person is an *am ha-aretz* . . . . R. Aḥa bar Yaakov said that he is a sorcerer [i.e., he practices sleight of hand]." Rashi explains the latter by saying that a person with superficial knowledge will utilize his knowledge to deceive people. In the same context, the Talmud says in the same passage: "R. Elazar said: 'He who teaches his daughter Torah is considered as if he had taught her *tiflut.*'"

But the precautions against superficial knowledge were balanced by another series of considerations. Whereas the Torah is not meant to be only an intellectual abstraction but is also meant to be realized in practice, the mitzvah of learning Torah is a dual one.[9] On its most basic level, it is derived from the verse "So that you will learn them and you will observe to keep them" (Deut. 5:1). One must study so that he will be able to perform. "The ignorant cannot be fearful of sin, nor can they be pious."[10] The law is exceedingly complex, and only one who is knowledgeable can be truly observant. Anyone who is truly motivated to observe the mitzvot will find himself equally motivated to study. The mitzvah of studying Torah extends far beyond the practical, however. The Torah is the word of God and hence valuable per se. All areas of Torah are significant, for they are all expressive of the divine will, whether or not they are relevant in practice.[11] Women are bound by the first commandment of studying Torah.[12] All who are bound to do are bound to know and understand what they are doing. The Tosafot[13] derive this rule from the verse in Deuteronomy, "Assemble the people, men, women, and children, and your stranger in your gates so that they will hear [understand] and so that they will learn and they will fear the Lord, your God, and they will be cautious to perform all the words of this Torah" (Deut. 31:12). In practice, therefore, women are dutybound to learn a large segment of the Torah, but they are not *required* to dedicate themselves completely to a total involvement in all aspects of the word of God.

The learning of Torah is an optional activity for women insofar as the command of intellectual involvement per se is concerned. However, if a woman does study Torah, she has a mitzvah, and her activity falls within the Talmud's discussion of the optional learning of Torah.

> R. Meir said: "How do we know that even a gentile who learns Torah is to be considered on a par with the high priest? It is because the verse in Scripture says: 'Which a *person* should do and live by them' [Lev. 18:5]. It does not say 'priest' or 'Levite' or 'Jew' but rather person. This teaches us that even a gentile who learns Torah is to be considered on the same level as a high priest." It was said [of R. Meir's statement] that he does not receive the reward of the obligated one but rather of a non-obligated performer [which is less], for R. Ḥanina said: "Greater is the reward of he who performs out of obligation than he who performs not out of obligation."[14]

The learning of Torah by women presents a paradox. On the one hand, it is a highly meritorious act.[15] On the other, it is an act frowned upon by R. Eliezer in the Mishnah. Maimonides quotes both sides of the paradox:

> A woman who studies Torah is rewarded, but not to the same degree as is a man, for she is not commanded and anyone who does that which he is not commanded to do, does not receive the same reward as one who is commanded but a lesser reward. However, even though she is rewarded, the sages commanded a man not to teach his daughter Torah. This is because women are not disposed to dedicate themselves to study and will turn the words of Torah into foolish words according to their limited understanding [due to their lack of interest]. Our sages said that anyone who teaches his daughter Torah is to be considered as if he had taught her trivial and unimportant things.[16]

The above phrase, "the sages commanded a man not to teach his daughter," was interpreted by R. Ḥayim Yosef David Azulay (d. 1806), commonly referred to as Ḥidah, as representing a practical warning rather than a legal prohibition.[17] He was puzzled by the fact that the Talmud describes positively the vast scholarship of Beruriah, the wife of R. Meir and daughter of R. Ḥananiah ben Teradion.[18] Had the command of the sages been a legal prohibition, then it would apply to all women equally, even to the most highly motivated and brilliant women. Ḥidah therefore concludes that the command of the sages is a warning against teaching women who are not sufficiently motivated. The sages recognized the fact that women were not involved in intellectual pursuits and cautioned against teaching them. This was not given the form of a legal prohibition and hence allowed motivated women to pursue their studies. Furthermore, it also allowed for a shift in attitude due to a change in the general orientation of women toward intellectual pursuits. A direct implication of Ḥidah's view would be that in contemporary society, where women are regularly involved in serious academic pursuits, they may, nay should, seriously pursue their Torah studies. The Talmud tells us that during the reign of Hezekiah, the religious and scholarly level of the people was so high that "they searched from Dan to Beer-Sheba and did not find an ignoramus, from Gevath to Antiproth and could not find a young boy or girl, man or woman, who was not completely conversant with the detailed laws of ritual cleanliness."[19] At times when motivation is high, the Torah is accessible to all alike, male and female.

The paradox is resolved in a different manner by the author of the *Perishah*[20] (d. 1640). To teach Torah to women is forbidden. However, if they demonstrate their motivation by studying Torah on their own, and thereby show that they consider it to be a serious pursuit, the prohibition is removed. Thus, even though he seems to give the statement "The sages commanded" a legal interpretation, he allows for a different attitude when we are confronted by a situation which clearly demonstrates motivation. One does not *impose* Torah knowledge upon women, as one does upon men, for they are not required to study. But one may teach Torah to a woman who demonstrates the proper motivation.

The view of Ḥidah and of the author of the *Perishah* is echoed in the responsa of R. Yehudah Aszod (d. 1866), who writes: "We do not find anywhere that women are forbidden to study."[21] In the volume of responsa, *Maayan Ganim,* the author not only permits motivated women to study the Torah but praises them and urges his audience to encourage them in their work.[22]

There is a small group of authorities who view "the command of the sages" as a legal prohibition.[23] However, even these scholars concur that this legal prohibition does not apply to the area of study required for performance. Everyone is of the opinion that such study is obligatory. The vast majority of scholars, on the other hand, have interpreted "the command of the sages" as a caution against teaching Torah to those who are not ready to take such studies seriously. However, at all times, even for these authorities, the study of Torah by women remains an optional activity.

A totally different direction has been taken by scholars of the twentieth century. Its effect has been to make Torah study mandatory for women. As has been seen, women are required to learn those areas of Torah necessary for the proper performance of their mitzvot. Rabbi Israel Meir ha-Cohen (d. 1933), author of *Ḥafetz Ḥayim,* in his work *Likutei Halakhot* to *Sotah,* comments on the talmudic statement regarding the learning of Torah by women:

> It would seem to me that this is only at those times of history when everyone lived in the place of his ancestors and the ancestral tradition was very strong for each individual and this motivated him to act in the manner of his forefathers. . . . However, nowadays, when the tradition of our fathers has become very weakened and we find people who do not live close to the parental environment and especially that there are those who have been given a secular education, certainly it is required to teach them the entire Bible, the ethical writings of our sages, etc., so that the principles of our holy faith will be strong for them. Otherwise, Heaven forbid, they may deviate entirely from the path of God, and violate all the precepts of the Torah.[24]

The author of *Hafetz Ḥayim* extends the requirement of teaching a woman those mitzvot which are applicable to her from practical instruction to include all that is necessary for proper motivation and performance. This, he says, varies from society to society. In those societies where the environment is sufficiently strong not to require education for proper motivation, no education is required, although it is permitted. However, in contemporary society, where education is a prerequisite for proper motivation, such education is not only permitted but is also required. Very few people with a college education in Western culture and a grade-school education in Judaism can be properly observant. For a college-educated woman, a college-level education in Judaism is not optional, it is absolutely required.

The words of the author of *Ḥafetz Ḥayim* are echoed by Rabbi Zalman Sorotzkin (d. 1966) in his work *Moznaim la-Mishpat.*[25] In an ingenious tour de force, he says that nowadays one who does not teach his daughter Torah leaves her prey to street culture and eo ipso teaches her its immorality. It is not the teaching of Torah that teaches *tiflut,* immorality, but rather the lack of such teaching.

The overwhelming weight of modern authority follows this line of reasoning,[26] and the existence of schools of higher Jewish learning for women among all factions of contemporary Orthodox Jewry is ample proof of this fact.

In summary, the learning of Torah is not obligatory for women as it is for men. A man's ultimate task is an all-engrossing involvement in the study of Torah. A woman's ultimate task is in another area and another direction. She is obligated to study and be proficient in order to perform her mandatory tasks. All knowledge necessary for the performance of her tasks is obligatory. At times when only technical knowledge is necessary, only technical knowledge is required. When more sophisticated knowledge is necessary to ensure performance, such knowledge is required. Other areas of knowledge are optional. The sages were cautious about permitting women to venture into areas irrelevant to performance. Some scholars say that they forbade it. Most say that they urged caution and prudence out of fear of the dangers of superficial knowledge. No authorities ever meant to justify the perverse modern-day situation in which women are allowed to become sophisticatedly conversant with all cultures other than their own. If, in the twentieth century, American women are more familiar with the Protestant ethic than with the Jewish ideal, it is nothing but a violation of the original intent of R. Eliezer's statement. In twentieth-century America, there is no reason for Jewish women to be ignorant of the basics of their tradition. All are dutibound to learn the word of God and serve Him.

The exclusion of women from Torah learning was not carried over to other areas of intellectual involvement. With reference to intellectual faculties the Talmud says: "R. Ḥisdah says . . . this teaches us that women were given greater intelligence *[binah yeterah]* than men."[27] Most commentaries have interpreted the talmudic statement in accordance with the above translation. Some have translated the key phrase *binah yeterah* as referring to earlier maturity.[28]

The current feminist critique of Judaism has seized upon another talmudic passage as an alleged denigration of the intelligence of women—the phrase *rov nashim daatan kalot alayhen.* According to feminist critics, this comment indicates that the talmudic sages regarded women as silly, frivolous, ignorant, and incapable of being educated. There is nothing in the Talmud to substantiate this claim.

The phrase is used twice in the Talmud, both times in the same context—that most women under intense pressure will yield more easily than most men.[29] This is not a general rule covering all situations and was never meant as such; it was only a statement of general psychological tendencies. Hence, we read *rov nashim*—"most women." It was never used in the Talmud in reference to intellectual abilities or moral character. To the contrary, in many places in the Bible and Talmud we find it asserted that woman is higher in a moral sense than man, as has been discussed earlier. The phrase *rov nashim daatan kalot alayhen* should be viewed in the context of the story we related earlier of the pious man and the pious woman.[30] While in a specific instance, under the pressure of the moment, a woman may yield more easily than a man, on a day-to-day-basis it is the woman who determines her husband's direction, for better or worse, rather than vice versa. Furthermore, this statement reflects the fact that women are generally more sensitive and softer than men. While to some contemporaries this may sound pejorative and an indication of an undesirable weakness, in the Jewish context it certainly refers to a positive trait of character. This trait allows women to excel in the field of *ḥesed*. Lastly, the said statement was *never* used by the Talmud or by *rishonim* in reference to the learning of Torah by women.

8

Women's Obligation in Mitzvot

There is virtually no distinction between men and women in the area of moral responsibility covered by the negative commandments,[1] except that three of the negative commandments are not applicable to women for technical reasons.[2] There is a distinction between men and women, however, in regard to the positive commandments. Women are obligated in virtually all positive commandments that are independent of time, but they are exempt from most, though not all, time-bound positive commandments.

It would be too facile, although perhaps not completely wrong, to say that women are excused from the time-bound commandments because of their familial responsibilities. Among the classic commentators, this opinion is found in the Abudrahm (d. 1345).[3] This view clearly points out the ultimacy of a woman's household tasks, as optional nonultimate tasks, however pressing, do not secure relief from ultimate responsibilities.[4] Most authorities disagree with the Abudrahm, many of them maintaining that he takes no cognizance of the fact that women who have no household tasks are also exempt from these mitzvot.[5] Most of the authorities offer no explanation for the exemption but regard it as part of the basic fabric of Jewish law to which the question "why?" is inapplicable. However, as the Talmud points out, the exemption implies nothing as to the relative worth of male and female[6]—both are equally sacred.

A few later authorities have taken the fact of women's exemption from various commandments as evidence of the greater ease with which women achieve spiritual goals. The

Maharal of Prague (d. 1609) views the exemption as reflective of the nature of woman's personality, which is naturally closer to the serenity necessary for spiritual achievement.[7] He writes that the performance of mitzvot and the learning of Torah are designed to enable human beings to achieve spiritual perfection. Man's aggression is a detriment to his spiritual aspirations and he therefore must work harder and be given extra religious tasks. Women, however, because of their greater potential for spiritual growth, require fewer mitzvot to achieve spiritual perfection. Thus, he says, the Talmud tells us that the reward promised to woman is greater than that promised to man.[8] It is assumed that they will generally achieve higher levels than men.[9]

Rabbi Samson Raphael Hirsch (d. 1888) writes that the nature of man's day-to-day activities requires extra mitzvot to provide him with the proper spiritual balance.

> The Torah did not impose those mitzvot on women because *it did not consider them necessary to be demanded from women.* All מצות עשה שהזמן גרמא, *mitzvot assei she'ha-zman grama,* are meant, by symbolic procedures, to being certain facts, principles, ideas and resolutions, afresh to our minds from time to time to spur us on afresh and to fortify us to realize them to keep them. God's Torah takes it for granted that our women have greater fervor and more faithful enthusiasm for their God-serving calling and that their calling runs less danger in their case than in that of men from the temptations which occur in the course of business and professional life. Accordingly, it does not find it necessary to give women those repeated spurring reminders to remain true to their calling, and warnings against weaknesses in their business lives.[10]

The exemption of women from time-bound positive commandments is a principle that exempts women from seven commandments: the recitation of the Shema, the wearing of tefillin, the wearing of tzitzit, the counting of the omer, hearing the shofar, dwelling in the sukkah, and taking the lulav. With the possible exception of tefillin, a woman is not barred from the performance of these commandments, only exempted. Most scholars have simply accepted the principle as a basic element of Jewish law; they have merely stated it without addressing themselves to the question "why?." A few have seen in this principle an implicit statement on the nature of woman's spiritual potential. No authority, in his evaluation of this principle, has quoted the following enigmatic midrashic statement.

> Why were women included with minors and slaves with regard to [their exemption from certain] mitzvot?* [It is] because of their single minded nature.† Thus it says: "And Hannah spoke of what was on her heart [mind]" [I Sam. 1:13]. "And I find more bitter than death the woman whose heart [mind] [places] snares and traps, her hands are as a prison. He who is good before God will be spared from her and a sinner shall be trapped by her" [Eccles. 7:26].‡ "And her husband arose and went after her to speak of what was on her heart [mind]" [Judg. 19:3]. Similarly of a minor the Bible says: "Foolishness is bound up in the heart [mind] of a child" [Prov. 22:15]. Similarly, a slave has a single-minded dedication to his master.[11]

Minors are exempted because they lack mature judgment and are single-minded in the pursuit of foolishness. Slaves are exempted because of their single-minded dedication to their masters, which precludes their dedicating themselves properly to the performance of mitzvot. A slave's time is not his own.

Unfortunately, the Midrash does not elaborate upon the nature of woman's single-mindedness and its implications for

*Technically, this is imprecise. Women and slaves are exempted from a limited number of mitzvot; minors from all of them.

†Literally, "because they have one heart."

‡The Talmud (*Yeb.* 63b) contrasts Solomon's picture of the evil wife with his view of the good wife: "He who has found a wife, has found goodness and receives favor from God" (Prov. 18:22).

mitzvot. The first verse cited by the Midrash concerns Hannah's single-minded preoccupation with her prayer; the second is concerned with the single-mindedness of an evil wife. The nature of the third biblical quotation is unclear. The Midrash does not suggest that there is a unifying factor behind the three biblical verses, nor is there any obvious explanation. Furthermore, the classic authorities do not make reference to this Midrash in their writings. While the statement of the Midrash is certainly consistent with the approaches of Abudrahm, Maharal, and Hirsch, it does not establish the validity of their analyses. The Midrash is also consistent with many other possible approaches. However, the total silence accorded this statement by all authorities seems to imply that they rejected it.

9

Women and Optional Mitzvot

Even though legislating one's own obligation is not generally permitted, a woman is allowed to perform optionally all the mitzvot from which she has been exempted. Furthermore, her optional performance is considered to be a meritorious act, i.e., a mitzvah, and not a mere irrelevant act. Rashi (d. 1105) is the only authority who suggests that there may be a problem in such optional acts.[1] In interpreting the talmudic discussion on whether or not women may put on tefillin, Rashi says that the argument revolves not only about tefillin but about all the mitzvot from which women have been exempted. R. Meir and R. Yehudah, who forbid performance of these *mitzvot,* base their view on the verse "Thou shalt not add or subtract" (Deut. 4:2, 13:1). One must worship God in the specific manner assigned to him and not choose alternative forms. It is not clear whether Rashi decides in favor of the above opinion or in favor of the opinion of R. Yossi, who, he says, permits women to perform all the mitzvot from which they have been exempted. All authorities, besides Rashi, clearly state that women perform virtually all the mitzvot from which they have been excused. Jewish practice is that women may perform all optional mitzvot with the exception of tallit and tefillin.

The *Magen Avraham* (d. 1683), however, suggests a legal mechanism through which women might actually become obligated in those mitzvot from which they have been exempted by the Torah.[2] The Talmud decided that ma'ariv, the evening prayer, is optional.[3] Most authorities say that since men have nonetheless taken the obligation of ma'ariv upon themselves, it is now obligatory for them. The *Magen Avraham* says that this is true of all optional mitzvot.[4] Thus, he says, women are obligated to count the omer because they have already accepted it upon themselves, and he would most probably extend this view to the mitzvot of shofar[5] and lulav, both of which are regularly performed by virtually all women. The reasoning of the *Magen Avraham*, however, is limited to optional mitzvot. It does not extend to the creation of new mitzvot. These may be religiously irrelevant or even possibly forbidden, but never obligatory. Furthermore, the obligation engendered by voluntary acceptance does not raise the mitzvah to the level of a divinely ordained mitzvah. The gap between human obligation and divine obligation is unbridgeable. Finally, the *Magen Avraham* does not speak of voluntary acceptance by an individual but rather by an entire community. If an individual accepted an optional mitzvah, it would most probably have the status of a personal *minhag* or a personal *neder*.

Virtually all the authorities agree that women may perform the mitzvot from which they have been exempted, but the question of whether they are permitted to recite the appropriate blessings is very controversial. Before performing a mitzvah, one must recite: "Blessed are You, O Lord, our God, King of the universe, who has sanctified us through his mitzvot and commanded us to . . . " The ending of the blessing depends on the specific mitzvah. The phrase "and commanded us" presents a problem in the case of optional mitzvot. Rabbenu Tam (d. 1171?) interpreted the phrase as referring to the collective obligation of the Jewish people,[6] and ruled that women, as part of the collective, could recite the blessing. Maimonides (d. 1204) interpreted the phrase as referring to individual obligation in the specific mitzvah and ruled that women could not recite the blessing when performing optional mitzvot.[7] Since the custom of Ashkenazic Jewry has been to follow Rabbenu Tam, Ashkenazic women recite blessings on optional mitzvot.[8]

Women are exempt from certain obligations. This does not exclude them from performing these mitzvot, but does reduce the meaningfulness of their performance. The value of a mitzvah lies in its divine command. To someone who views Judaism as the ultimate ego trip, the inability to perform certain male tasks may be severely debilitating. However, that is just the point. The essence of Judaism is for a Jew to live his life in conjunction with the divine will.[9] For a male, it is the divine imperative to a male. For a female, it is the divine imperative to a female. For a priest, it is the divine imperative to a priest. For a Levite, it is the divine imperative to a Levite. For an Israelite, it is the divine imperative to him.

Part of a Jew's morning prayer is the recitation of a series of blessings: "who has not created me a gentile," "who has not created me a slave," "who has not created me a woman." In place of the last blessing, women recite the blessing "who has created me in accordance with His will." The source for the above prayer for men is the Tosefta, which reads:

> R. Yehudah said: "A man must recite every day . . . 'Blessed art Thou . . . who has not made me a woman' . . . for women are not commanded in [all of the][10] mitzvot."[11]

A man acknowledges his extra duties every morning through these blessings.

The recitation of a blessing marks a phenomenon which reminds the individual of God's actions in this world. Sometimes blessings are expressions of gratitude, *birkot hodo'oh.* Sometimes they are statements of praise and recognition of God's activity, *birkot shevaḥ.* Before one eats anything, he recites a blessing acknowledging God as the source of mankind's sustenance. This is a *birkat shevaḥ.* After one eats, he expresses gratitude for the food he has eaten. This is a *birkat hodo'oh.* When a close relative dies, one recites a blessing recognizing and accepting God's judgment and infinite wisdom. When one beholds thunder and lightening, he recites a blessing acknowledging and praising God as the ordainer of the laws of nature. The last two blessings are *birkot shevaḥ.*

Some authorities have interpreted the morning blessings as *birkhot shevaḥ.* Rabbi Samson Raphael Hirsch writes:

> This is not a prayer of thanks that God did not make us heathens, slaves, or women. Rather it calls upon us to contemplate that task which God has imposed upon us by making us free Jewish men, and to pledge ourselves to do justice to this mission. These three aspects of our own status impose upon us duties much more comprehensive than the rest of mankind. And if our women have a smaller number of mitzvot to fulfill than men, they know that the tasks which they must discharge as free Jewish women are no less in accordance with the will and desire of God than are those of their brothers. Hence their blessing is "who has created me in accordance with His will."[12]

Most commentators have interpreted these blessings as *birkot hodo'oh.* From this perspective, the blessings are a man's expression of gratitude to God for providing him with extra opportunities to serve God—not gratitude for a higher station in life, but for fourteen extra opportunities to serve Him.

The woman, when reciting her blessing, acknowledges that the role differentiation implicit in her exemption from certain mitzvot is part of the overall divine plan for the world, whose justification lies in the will and wisdom of God.

Certain recent authorities have made much of the fact that all the blessings are in the negative form, while the woman's special blessing is in the affirmative.[13] The standard interpretation of the negative form is that it would have been better for man not to have been created than to have been created.[14] The difficulties and trials of life are at times so overwhelming that the negative aspects of life very often outweigh the positive ones. However, this does not grant us the license to resign from life.[15] True, it might have been better for man not to have been created. But now that he has been created, he must seek ways of enriching and infusing value into his existence. Thus one recites the blessings regarding his creation in the negative, not the positive.

Why, then, does a woman recite her blessings in the positive? It has been suggested that the blessing for women thanks God for a different aspect of creation—for having created woman's nature similar to God's will. We relate to God in his role of enabler and as the archetype of the performer of *ḥesed.* These are represented by the creation of woman in a greater sense than the creation of man. Thus women say: "Who has made me similar to His will."

Much has recently been written in the feminist press about the supposed disparagement of women through their exemption from time-bound positive commandments. The basic thrust of the critique has been that the exemption of women from positive time-bound commandments equates them with slaves,[16] thereby insulting their human dignity and rendering their Judaism peripheral. This is nothing but a classic example of the "like result implies like cause" fallacy of reasoning. It is true that a slave is an incomplete Jew, in the sense that he undergoes a voluntary conversion ceremony before he can be held permanently.[17] The incomplete conversion ceremony renders him a partial Jew, and his partial obligation in mitzvot is indicative of this status. Maimonides says: "Slaves who have immersed themselves for conversion and accepted upon themselves those mitzvot which are obligatory on slaves have left the status of non-Jew and not yet reached the status of Jew."[18] Thus, a free slave requires an additional conversion ceremony to complete his Judaism.[19] This is so whether the slave is male or female.[20]

The Torah often uses the word *aḥiv,* which is interpreted by the Talmud as meaning a completely obligated Jew.[21] Both slaves and non-Jews are excluded by this reference.[22] A woman is not excluded by *aḥiv.*[23] There is a fundamental difference between the exemption of slaves from positive time-bound commandments and that of women. The exemption of slaves stems from the fact that their conversion is incomplete and hence so is their degree of obligation. A woman, however, is a completely obligated Jew, and her exemption is not an indication of an incomplete status as a Jew. Thus a woman is included in the status of *aḥiv* while a slave is not. Furthermore, had the equation of woman with slave been actually true, the personal status of a Jewish woman and a slave woman would be exactly the same. However, a slave woman, upon being freed, requires an additional conversion ceremony in order to pass from the status of incomplete Jewess to the status of complete Jewess.

Lastly, one should remember that in Jewish thought every human life is sacred, and no one can judge the relative value of one human life over another. This principle finds expression in the law that if one is presented with the option of kill or be killed, he must not kill.[24] The Talmud explains that it is not in the hands of any mortal to judge the relative value of one human life against another.[25] This law applies equally to male and female, Jew and non-Jew, slave and free man.

The contemporary feminist critique of Judaism has seen the exemption of women from time-bound positive commandments as a serious handicap to spiritual achievement. A characteristic article expressing this attitude is "The Jew Who Wasn't There" by Rachel Adler.[26] Adler claims that the restriction imposed upon women by these exemptions, in practical terms, deprives them of the right to participate in the fundamental areas of religious self-expression. "In other words, members of this category have been 'excused' from most of the positive symbols which for the male Jew hallow time, hallow his physical being and inform both his myth and his philosophy." While this may sound fine, a closer look at the record does not bear out her thesis. Both women and men are required to pray, the basic difference between them being that women are required to pray twice a day, men three times. The third prayer, ma'ariv, the evening prayer, is also optional for men.[27] However, they have accepted it upon themselves and rendered it obligatory. It is a most specious form of reasoning to find within this self-imposed exemption a pejorative posture. There are eleven major and minor holidays during the year. The most important one is the Sabbath. This is also the one with the most fundamental impact on the life of the Jew. There is no distinction whatsoever between men and women as far as the mitzvah of the Sabbath is concerned.[28] Among the occasional holidays, Yom Kippur, the Day of Atonement, probably does more than any other to establish and cultivate a Jew's relationship with God. There is no distinction whatsoever between men and women as far as the mitzvah of the Day of Atonement is concerned.[29] The Passover holiday, in all of its details, both the negative aspects of not eating ḥametz and the positive aspects of the entire seder symbolism and the holiday aspect of the first two and last two days, is equally incumbent upon men and upon women. There is no distinction whatsoever between men and women as far as the mitzvah of Passover is concerned.[30] The same applies to the mitzvah of Shevuot.[31] The mitzvah of Ḥannukah is applicable to both men and women since it embraces all who were involved in the miracle.[32] The same applies to Purim with all of its commandments.[33] The fast days, with their positive and negative aspects, are also applicable to men and women alike.[34] Rosh Ḥodesh is more applicable to women than to men. It was given to women as an optional holiday in reward for their extra piety as evidenced by their refusal to participate in the making of the golden calf.[35] Shemini Atzeret is a holiday for men and women equally.[36] The only holidays where a distinction is drawn between men and women are Rosh HaShannah and Sukot. While women are commanded to observe both holidays, they are excused from the special holiday rituals, i.e., hearing the shofar,[37] dwelling in the Sukah,[38] and taking the lulav.[39] These three acts are optional for women, and to the best of my knowledge, most observant women perform all of them. Thus, to say that women are not given the opportunity to hallow time through the appropriate ritual really takes very little cognizance of the facts.

The other area of time-bound positive commandments from which women are excused are those which reflect a day-night difference, i.e., tallit,[40] tefillin,[41] and Shema.[42] As important as these are, I really find it a little preposterous to say that they are the exclusive or even major means of religious self-expression, as Adler would like to maintain. Furthermore, the one really "denied" to women is tefillin,[43] which, although important, is certainly not the central ritual in Judaism.

Adler says: "Since most of the *mitzvot* not restricted by time are negative, and since women, children and slaves are responsible to fulfill all negative *mitzvot,* including the negative time-bound *mitzvot,* it follows that for members of this category, the characteristic posture of their Judaism is negation rather than affirmation." The reason that most mitzvot not restricted by time are negative is that most mitzvot in general are negative. This is true for both men and women. There are 365 negative commanments and 248 positive ones. There are essentially only fourteen positive commandments from which women are excused: (1) the reading of the Shema twice daily; (2) learning and teaching Torah, (3) putting tefillin on the head, (4) putting tefillin on the arm, (5) placing tzitzit on four-cornered garments, (6) writing a Torah, (7) recitation of the priestly blessings by male priests, (8) counting the omer (this is problematic, since Naḥmanides obligates women in the counting of the omer), (9) dwelling in the sukkah, (10) taking the lulav, (11) hearing the shofar, (12) procreation, (13) circumcision, (14) making one's wife happy during the first year of marriage. Furthermore, the claim that the negative commands contain only negation and not affirmation depends very much on one's posture. Kashrut is a negative command. However, it can be an affirmative element of the Jewish experience. The *Mekhiltah* tells us:

> "Saying," this teaches us that the Jews answered to the positive commands yes and to the negative commands no. These are the words of R. Yishmael. R. Akiva taught that on the positive commandments they answered yes and on the negative ones they also answered yes.[44]

The essence of R. Akiva's answer to R. Yishmael is that affirmation also exists within the negative commandments.

Adler's further position that a woman is bound to comply with the negative mitzvot so as not to undermine Jewish life is baseless. First of all, this does not take into account that women are bound by nearly all the positive commands. Why would a woman undermine Jewish life more by not praying than by not saying the Shema? A woman is commanded in all the essential "duties of the heart" of love and fear of God which direct and command man to engage in a relationship with God.[45] Adler would have done well to remember the verse in Psalms read in the Friday night service: "The daughters of Zion exult in their King [i.e., God] because of your commands, O God!" (Ps. 97:8). Does this sound like a denial of women maintaining a positive relationship with God? A woman may keep kosher so that her family can keep kosher, but she is also commanded to keep kosher as a unique individual.

Adler continues: "It was, perhaps, most damaging that the woman's meager *mitzvot* are, for the most part, closely connected to some physical goal or object." This statement misses the whole point of the mitzvot. There are two distinct types of mitzvot: duties of the heart, and mitzvot which revolve around physical objects. Women are excused from the Shema,[46] but this is the only duty of the heart from which they are excused. Women are commanded to know God, love Him, and fear Him, to declare His unity to sanctify His Name, and to pray to Him.[47] Among the mitzvot which revolve about physical objects, most concern the physical objects of everyday life, and a few, but only a few, concern ritual objects. A famous Midrash tells us that the angels requested that the Torah be given to them.[48] God answered that the essential part of the Torah revolves about the physical objects and activities in man's everyday life and is therefore inapplicable to angels. The Torah is for man involved in the physical world, not for ethereal spiritual beings. It orders the way he dresses, eats, conducts business, farms, cuts his hair, and a myriad of other activities. The Torah suffuses the physical with the spiritual. The physical and the spiritual are not antagonistic to the Jew. They are to be joined and welded together by both men and women. To identify men with the spiritual and women with the physical, and hence to denigrate the woman, comes close to Christianity but has no place in Judaism.

Adler concludes with a three-pronged complaint against contemporary and classic rabbinic leadership. First, their answers do not accept her as a person and set rigid stereotypes which define her by limiting the directions in which she may grow. Second, they are dishonest, for they do not proceed from a halakhic, but rather from a metahalakhic or non-halakhic, point of view. Third, they have stagnated and not been responsive to the cries of oppressed womanhood.

The first complaint is analyzed in chapter 3. The second critique misses the whole point of the halakhic approach. The strict halakhist makes no judgments or value statements with regard to the law. The law is the law, nothing more. It is the given means for serving God and for achieving personal value. Once one steps outside the law and proceeds with an analysis like Adler's, which is decidedly nonhalakhic, a halakhic answer cannot be expected. Halakhic answers exist for halakhic questions. Nonhalakhic questions must receive nonhalakhic answers.

Third, the claim of alleged insensitivity to the cry of oppressed womanhood takes very little cognizance of the nature of the halakhic process. Certain statements are absolute, and no amount of petitions will convince a serious and sincere halakhic scholar to change his mind, if the Halakhah says otherwise. A serious scholar realizes that the law is God's, not his.[49] A scholar's task is merely to communicate honestly the word of God.

Many statements, of course, are more flexible and have always been so interpreted. The total change in attitude of halakhic scholars on the issue of educating women certainly demonstrates that flexibility is possible when it is consistent with the Halakhah. Halakhic scholars have always approached their task with open minds and empathy, but also with a complete realization that the Torah is the word of God and must be treated as such. They never have viewed women as the tools to do mitzvot, as Adler claims, but as unique Jewish souls striving to know God and to serve Him. This has been the basis of the Jewish attitude toward women and will always continue to be. Both men and women together strive for self-transcendence. The Jewish woman has never been a *golem*, but rather a singular being endowed by God with a divine image and given by Him the means and the tasks to develop that image. Both men and women find their ultimate value and meaning as עבדי ה׳, servants of God.

10

Nonhalakhic Approaches to the Divine

The inability to perform certain mitzvot may at times inhibit the drive to achieve closeness to God, and it may then seem that other means of service are more religiously meaningful. What, in the Jewish view, is the validity of a humanly designed pattern to realize the goal of confronting the divine? Certainly, human legislation lacks the ultimacy of the divine word, nor can human legislation dispense with divine obligation. The right to divine legislation clearly rests exclusively with God. Is there any meaning, however, to a totally human initiative?

Two stories in the Bible warn us of the great danger implicit in nonhalakhic approaches to the divine. One concerns Nadab and Abihu, the eldest sons of Aaron, the high priest. The dedication of the Tabernacle was an occasion of great ritual ceremony and rejoicing. Nadab and Abihu, however, who are described in the midrash[1] as considering themselves to be superior servants of God,[2] felt inhibited by the ceremonial restrictions imposed on them as priests. While the priests were to participate in the entire ceremony of dedication, they were not permitted to place the fire on the altar. Nadab and Abihu, sincerely hoping to serve God in a superior fashion, wished to place the fire on the altar. To intensify their religious devotion, they prepared themselves by drinking wine. They then entered the Tabernacle. "And Nadab and Abihu, the sons of Aaron, each took his own pan and placed in it incense and fire, and they offered to God a strange fire which He had not commanded them. And a fire came forth from God and consumed them, and they died in front of God" (Lev. 10:1–2). Lest the message be lost, Moses spelled it out in detail in the next verse. All Jews, even those who consider themselves to be the most high and holy, can only serve God in the manner prescribed. God wants neither extra forbidden offerings nor artificially stimulated devotion. No matter how lofty the motivation to do otherwise, we must conform to all the set rules for divine service.

The same idea is expressed in a biblical story about King Saul. Before Saul went into battle, Samuel commanded him to kill the entire flock of the Amalekites. Upon his return from battle, Saul told Samuel that he had violated the command to kill the flock so that he could bring them as sacrifices to God. Samuel chastised Saul: "Does God have as great delight in burnt offerings and sacrifices as in listening to the voice of God? Behold, listening is preferable to a sacrifice, to pay attention is preferable to the fat of rams" (1 Sam. 15:22). No matter how lofty man's goal, divine service must be performed within the context of divine law. All attempts at human legislation must take cognizance of this limitation and not confuse themselves with divine legislation.

A more essential question concerns the meaningfulness and permissibility of ceremonies and rituals which do not violate any specific precept of the Torah.[3] The Torah states twice: "Thou shalt not add or subtract" (Deut. 4:2, 13:1). Some authorities have interpreted this restriction as limiting the ability to change existing ritual objects, i.e., tefillin, tzitzit, etc.[4] The Torah determines the nature of ritual objects. Maimonides (d. 1204) and Naḥmanides (d. 1270) extend the prohibition to new ceremonies and rituals.

Maimonides says that the prohibition limits the rights of a legally constituted beth-din.[5] Under certain well-defined circumstances, a beth-din has the legislative prerogative of enacting laws whose purpose is to ensure the proper observance of the mitzvot—the famous "fence around the Torah."[6]

This legislative power is limited in two directions. "Thou shalt not subtract" prevents the elimination of a mitzvah, even if the elimination is intended for the apparent betterment of divine service. "Thou shalt not add" informs us that any valid legislation by the beth-din must be identified as such. The line between divine and human legislation must never be blurred—it must always be clear and obvious.

Naḥmanides, on the other hand, interprets the verse as applying to any new ritual, introduced by an individual. The mitzvot of the Torah are the only acceptable ritual means of divine service. All forms of divine service must be expressed through the rituals and ceremonies defined by the Torah. "In my opinion, even if a person wishes to create a new mitzvah, for instance to make a holiday in a month that he chooses, as was done by Jeroboam, it is a violation of this prohibition."[7]

While Naḥmanides' interpretation of the verse "Thou shalt not add" is accepted by only a few authorities, his view on non-obligated mitzvot is accepted almost universally. The Talmud says: "R. Ḥanina said: 'Greater is the reward of one who performs mitzvot under obligation than one who performs them optionally.'"[8] Ritva (d. 1340) comments:

> Our great teacher [Naḥmanides] has explained that mitzvot are not done for the benefit of God, who commanded them, but for our own merit. One who is obligated and acts in conformity with divine obligation is therefore more greatly rewarded than the one who does not act out of a response to divine obligation. However, even he is rewarded. He, out of the goodness and piety of his heart, has gone and done the commandments of God. But one who does rituals which are not part of the Torah at all is referred to by the saying of the sages,[9] "One who is excused from a matter and performs it is called a *hedyot*, a common ignoramus."[10]

The introduction of new rituals may not be absolutely forbidden, but it is certainly an exercise in futility, a series of meaningless activities. Furthermore, the Talmud Yerushalmi indicates that acting like a *hedyot* is simply not allowed.[11] The pursuit of irrelevant and meaningless ritual is to be discouraged because it is a diversion from essential, meaningful activity. Furthermore, it lessens the significance of truly ultimate activity.

Since it is clearly appropriate for Jews to thank God for all the good He has given them, it is certainly permissible to celebrate the birth of a daughter or her bat-mitzvah.[12] However, it completely mocks the entire structure of Judaism to invest these celebrations with specific and detailed rituals. A few examples will elucidate this point.

The first Friday night of a baby boy's life is marked by a celebration called a *shalom zakhor*. Traditionally, there is no corresponding celebration for a girl (*shalom nekevah* or *simḥat bat*). The reasoning is simple and clear. A *shalom zakhor* is a prelude to the circumcision, the *brit milah*. There are two main reasons for this celebration. The Midrash says that a baby must experience the sanctity of the Sabbath before he can be sanctified through circumcision.[13] The *shalom zakhor* celebrates this initial sanctification. Secondly, the Talmud tells us that during Roman times, a celebration was made on the Sabbath subsequent to a boy's birth in the hope of distracting the attention of the Romans from the circumcision ceremony, forbidden by Roman law, that would be conducted on the eighth day.[14] While it is certainly in order to celebrate the birth of a daughter, a *shalom nekevah* or *simhat bat* destroys the meaning of the *shalom zakhor*. Imitation of male ceremonies is not necessary to make women feel significant.

An even more ridiculous ceremony, often refered to as a *britah*, has recently been introduced on the eighth day of a girl's life. It too is invested with a detailed ritual. In some places, the blessing of *koret habrit*, "maker of the covenant," is recited without mentioning God's name. This ceremony mocks the very concept of *brit*. A *brit*, or covenant, cannot be unilateral, it must be bilateral. Thus Abraham performed all the mitzvot of the Torah without a specific command, but he did not circumcise himself until God issued a specific command. Circumcision, a sign of the covenant, cannot be initiated by man. God, and God alone, initiates covenants with man. A unilaterally executed covenant with God is, at best, a meaningless form of spiritual autoeroticism. Finally the Talmud tells us that a woman becomes a member of the covenant automatically at birth.[15] Thus, to insist that a woman needs a form of spiritual self-stimulation to enter into the covenant is to place her on a lower level than classical Judaism has viewed her.

Many other examples could be cited. Creative divine service may or may not be forbidden, but it is certainly meaningless and should be discouraged. To pursue ritual creativity is to deny divine obligation as the source of all meaning in religious activity.

A Jew does not view his Judaism as the cultural expression of a patriarchal society which imposes artificial sex-role differentiation on unwilling womanhood. Rather, Jewish law is the divinely given way through which each individual tries, in his own unique manner, to achieve closeness to the divine source. All human lives are equivalent in value, and no greater value is attributed to the masculine role than to the feminine. While the male role may, because of its public nature, seem more glamorous, the female role is equally important and equally valued. Women are not viewed as mundane beings in contrast to men who are spiritual beings. Both men and women were created in the image of God, and both are enjoined to develop their individual divine image to its maximum. Jewish woman is not woman put on an ivory-tower pedestal by man. She is an equal partner in man's life work, and it is only through their joint work that a true Jewish life can be lived and Jewish survival be guaranteed.

PART II

The Legal Issue

11

Law and Judaism

The Halakhah, the moral laws of the Torah, like the physical laws of the natural world, derives its ultimate validation from its divine origin. The compelling feature of the moral law lies in the fact that it expresses the divine will. Man satisfies his existential need for value by responding to this expression of the divine will, because Jewish law is the divinely ordained way through which each individual is enabled, in his own unique manner, to achieve closeness to the divine source.

In a way, Jewish law is the solution to the question that Kierkegaard poses in *Sickness Unto Death:* "The majority of men live without being thoroughly conscious that they are spiritual beings, and to this is referable all their security, contentment with life, etc., etc. . . . Those, on the other hand, who say that they are in despair are generally such as have a nature so much more profound, that they become conscious of themselves as spirit. . . . That a sparrow can exist is comprehensible; it does not know anything about existing before God. But to know that one exists before God—and then not to go crazy or be brought to naught,"[1] how is that possible? When man stops to contemplate the unbridgeable chasm that separates him from God, the very source of his value, he can do nothing else but shrink in despair. This is exactly where Jewish law begins to function in the Jewish religious experience. Jewish law is the response to the question, "*How* do I exist before God?" Man achieves value by his response to the divine will. Each man achieves his unique value by his unique response to the divine will.[2] As was discussed in detail in the first section, God is the sole arbiter of moral action because He is the sole source of our value. He is *the* source of Jewish axiology. He who is the source of our physical reality is the source of our sense of value. Thus, in the realm of axiology, the question "why?" is not the essential question, because the essence of the moral imperative is the divine will, and beyond that there is no why. The moral "why?" like the physical "why?" is nothing but the search for the underlying principles of the divine will.

Judaism is thoroughly legal from beginning to end. If, to the linguistic philosopher, reality is ultimately language, and reality is important and meaningful to the extent that it can be expressed in language, to the Jew, reality is ultimately law. The moral ethic is important to the degree that it can be expressed in terms of law.

12

Letter and Spirit of the Law

The Jewish emphasis on law is at the very root of the conflict between Judaism and Christianity. Christianity grated at the Jewish insistence on law and tried to free the doctrines of love and kindness, so beautifully developed in Judaism, from their legal bounds. This thrust must be viewed within the perspective of the basically Greek origins of Christianity. One of the principal ideas that winds its way through Greek philosophy is the dichotomy between ideal form and concrete particulars. For Plato there was a dichotomy between the Platonic ideal of the table and the specific table experienced by the senses. The concrete table was the imperfect representation of the ideal table. True knowledge pertained to the ideal table, not the concrete table. True knowledge in all areas concerned the Ideas, not particulars. Knowledge of concrete things is of a lesser nature than knowledge of the Ideas. While Aristotle may have rejected the Platonic doctrine of Ideas, the dichotomy appears in his thought in the distinction between form and concrete particulars. In fact, by the time of the rise of Christianity, Plato's doctrine of Ideas had permeated the Hellenistic world and to some degree colored almost every type of thought.[1] Consequently, the body/soul dichotomy developed: the body was the prison of the soul; the soul was man's noble essence; therefore, the soul was to be glorified and the body denied.

While Plato stopped short of asceticism, the following speech in the *Phaedo* is surely typical. "Ought the philosopher to care about the pleasure of eating and drinking and what about the pleasures of love and will he think much about the other ways of indulging the body? Would you not say that he is entirely concerned with the soul and not with the body? The philosopher's whole life has been a rehearsal for death." Plato stopped here. The Gnostics took the doctrine all the way to asceticism. Thus, latter-day Platonists, Pythagoreans, and many early Christians encouraged flight from worldly affairs and hatred of the body. To Paul, and many others, abstinence was the ideal, and married life a concession to man's baser nature.[2]

When later thinkers applied this dichotomy to the legal sphere, it resulted in the split between the letter of the law and the spirit of the law.[3] Just as for Plato true knowledge pertained to the ideals and the essence of man was the soul, to the exclusion of the body, so too in Christianity the essential task of man was seen in terms of the spirit of the law.

Far from this dualism, so ingrained in the Greek mind, was the Jewish perception of reality. Jews never dealt very much in the metaphysical, so there is no well-developed doctrine in that area. As regards the body/soul dichotomy, the Jew sees body and soul as a closely knit unit. Each complements the other; each colors the other. Death is not a goal, as it was for Socrates, but rather the Jew fears death.[4] "What profit is there to me, when I go down into destruction? Will dust praise you? Will it relate your truths?" (Ps. 39:10). "For in death there is no remembrance of You. In Sheol who can praise You?" (Ps. 6:6). Death is a dissolution of the basic unit of life—the union of body and soul. Body without soul decays; soul without body is static.[5] "The dead do not praise God" (Ps. 115:17). Judaism is made for this world, where body and soul function together as one unit.

In the legal area also, for Judaism there is no split between letter and spirit. They comprise one unit, and neither exists without the other. Both the letter of the law and the spirit of the law derive their validation from the divine will. The spirit of the law does not justify the law, since both rely on the same source for their justification. There is no independent validation of the spirit of the law.[6]

What is the relationship in Judaism between the letter of the law and the spirit of the law? Here we find an interesting controversy between R. Shimon and his colleagues. The Bible says: "Do not pervert the justice of the stranger or of the orphan, and do not take as security for a loan the clothing of the widow" (Deut. 24:17). No reason is given for this law, nor is any distinction drawn between different types of widows. The Talmud says: "The security cannot be collected either from a rich widow or from a poor one, says R. Judah. R. Shimon says the security may be collected from a rich widow and not from a poor one."[7] The Talmud proceeds to analyze the disagreement, stating that R. Shimon is of the opinion that the moral background of the law must be made part of the law itself.[8] This is not to say that R. Shimon rejects the concept of law, but rather he insists that the moral underpinnings of the law must be introduced into the legal structure itself—they cannot remain extralegal. R. Judah disagrees—no matter how transparent the moral background may be, as long as the Bible did not introduce it into the legal structure, it must remain outside the legal structure. Every legal system must draw a sharp distinction between the motivation for the law and the law itself. The opinion of R. Shimon is rejected and the opinion of R. Judah is accepted as the majority opinion.

But does this mean that R. Judah rejects any moral basis for the law and holds that the law is merely the law? Here we must refer to another section of the Talmud. The Bible says that one must not pluck out the eggs from underneath the mother bird.[9] In reference to this, the Mishnah says: "He who says in his prayer 'He who has mercy on the nest of the bird [have mercy on us]' is to be silenced."[10] The Talmud asks for an explanation of the above and says:

> The reason for this was debated by two amoraim [scholars of the talmudic period] from Israel, R. Yosi bar Avin and R. Yosi

> bar Zvida. One of them said that the reason for silencing him is that this statement implies that God is partial to certain members of creation [i.e., it implies that God has mercy on birds but not on others]. One of them said that he is silenced because God's command is not given out of mercy, but is a mere decree.[11]

There have been two distinct approaches to this passage, one of which is most clearly exemplified by Naḥmanides,[12] and the other by Maimonides in the *Moreh Nevukhim*.[13] Both amoraim, Naḥmanides says, see a moral basis to the law in general. The difference of opinion is only in determining the basis for the specific law in question. The first scholar maintains that God exhibits mercy to all creatures, even to animals. The other says that God's mercy extends only to human beings, but that it is in man's best interest to act mercifully to animals, for this will condition him to act mercifully to other human beings. According to Naḥmanides, no one has ever said that there is no moral basis to the law.

Maimonides, however, saw in this controversy a more fundamental issue. The essence of the problem, he says, is whether or not there is a moral basis to the law.

The second opinion in the Talmud is that the laws are nothing but the expression of divine will into which we should not read more than is explicitly stated. The letter of the law is the spirit of the law. The first view concurs that the justification for the law lies, not in any underlying moral judgment, but rather in the divine will. But this does not prevent us from seeing within these laws certain moral principles also deriving their validity from the divine will. True, the divine will may seem arbitrary, and in fact this is very often the case, but we must not readily assume that it is.

Although the Talmud does not decide between the two views—practical issues are pressing and are generally resolved, philosophic issues are not so pressing and are generally left unresolved—Maimonides accepts the first view in the Talmud.[14]

Elaborating on this theme,[15] he maintains that both the physical and the moral worlds derive their existence from divine creation. Divine will brought both into being. In both areas one cannot ask "why?" because if one gave an underlying principle explaining why, he would then be faced with the same question regarding the new principle, and so on. Divine will justifies itself. The divine wisdom can be analyzed, but not the divine will. We can determine the sun's function in creation and how that function is achieved, but why God created the sun and why he deemed its function necessary cannot be determined. We can ask "how?" but not "why?."

So, too, in the moral sphere we ask "how?" not "why?." All the commands in the Torah function toward two ends—perfecting man's physical life, and perfecting his spiritual life. Perfecting his physical life is also a means to the perfection of his spiritual life—the only real end of the Torah. The search for underlying principles is the search for an understanding of the way the mitzvot function toward that end.

As much as Maimonides insisted on the importance of the search for underlying principles, still he injected a word of caution in a most beautiful and characteristic fashion. In the concluding section of the laws of *Meilah** he says:

> It is fitting for a man to ponder the laws of the holy Torah and to comprehend their full meaning to the extent of his ability. Nevertheless, a law for which he finds no reason and for which he sees no cause should not be trivial in his eyes. Let him not "break forth to rise up against the Lord, lest the Lord break forth upon him,"[16] and let him not think about the Torah in the same manner as he thinks about secular and everyday matters. Let us see how strict the Torah was with the crime of *Meilah*. Now, if wood and stones, earth and ashes, just because a man has designated them for use in the Temple, by speech alone, have become sanctified and anyone who treats them in an or-

**Meilah* is the crime of using for one's own personal use an object that has been designated for end in the service in the Temple.

> dinary everyday manner has committed the crime of *Meilah*, and even if he did this unintentionally he requires atonement, how much more should a man be on guard not to rebel against a commandment decreed for us by the Almighty, only because he does not understand the reason, nor should he ascribe incorrect things to God, nor should he regard the commandments as ordinary affairs.[17]

The treatment of sacred as profane, of the sacrosanct as everyday, can have devastating consequences.[18] The ascription of underlying moral motifs to the divine imperative should not allow one to sit in judgment, but rather to deepen his own understanding. Rabbi Samson Raphael Hirsch offers a clear statement of this.

> Such speculation and attempts at inquiry into the motives behind these laws would be a presumptuous and dangerous undertaking for a person who does not cleave to God's commandments simply because they are His, but who makes his belief in their sanctity and binding force subject to the results of his investigation into their reason and purposes. Such inquiry on the part of him in whose heart אמונה במצות ה' *emunah be'mitzvot hashem* [commitment to the *mitzvot* of God] does not take precedence over his speculation upon them would be a fatal venture indeed. It should be remembered that a person of this mentality is not led to defection through his speculation, for he has already set aside the אמונה במצות *emunah be'mitzvot* [commitment to *mitzvot*] long before he has ever crossed the threshold to the hall of thought and inquiry. The request in this Psalm for better understanding and insight, therefore, bases itself upon an avowal in the words כי האמנתי במצותיך *kee he'amanti be'mitzvotekha* [for I am committed to your *mitzvot*]; his אמונה במצותיך *emunah bemitzvotekha* [commitment to your *mitzvot*] is not to be based upon such insight and understanding, but should precede the latter and form the granite foundation for whatever investigation he might undertake. The sole reason why he seeks to inquire into the word of God is that, to him, the divine commandments are indeed the Law of the

> Lord, and hence, by inquiring into them, he seeks to investigate the trail of Divine wisdom, even as the human mind endeavors to search the marvels of nature and history for the demonstration of God's wisdom and almighty power. And he prays: גל עיני ואביטה נפלאות מתורתיך *gal aynai ve'abitah niflaot mi'Toratekha* "Open Thou my eyes, that I may behold miracles from Thy Law." (Psalms 119:18).[19]

This point of view creates a fundamental difference in attitude between Jewish law and common law. Common law, or any other humanly devised system, begins with a specific social system and social goals and then devises a logical means to ensure the maximal achievement of that social order. The validity of the legal system is judged by the degree to which it furthers the social order it set out to achieve. The point of view comes first and then comes the law. This concept has no place in the Halakhah. Each individual Halakhah has its own individual validation, derived from the fact of its divine origin rather than from its efficacy as a means to some social, moral, or religious end. The sociological results of the system can be evaluated, but this is always post facto and can never become the basis for an evaluation of a specific Halakhah or of a complex of Halakhot. The world view of Torah and the social order of Jewish society are determined post facto after the completion of a halakhic discussion. This is essential to the entire halakhic process.[20]

13

Women as Witnesses

One of the areas of Jewish law most misunderstood by feminist critics is the disqualification of women as witnesses in Jewish courts. Certain critics[1] have claimed that women are put in the same category as deaf mutes, the insane, and minors,* or what is worse, as gamblers, usurers, and pigeon-racers.†

Nothing could be more absurd. The fundamental fact underlying the entire Jewish law regarding witnesses and evidence is that knowledge beyond the shadow of a doubt is not itself sufficient to convict. The concept of *edut,* witnessed testimony, has many technical requirements far beyond the mere requirements of credibility. The Talmud tells us:

> We have learnt that R. Shimon ben Shetaḥ said: "I once saw a man running after his friend into a deserted area and I ran after him and found a sword in his hand and blood dripping and a man killed, and I said: 'Evil man, who killed this man, either you or I, but what can I do, for your life is not given into my hands, for behold the Torah said, "According to the statement of two or three witnesses shall the convicted one die" [Deut. 17:6], but the Almighty will extract payment from you.'" Before R. Shimon left, a snake came and bit the man and he died.[2]

*Minors, deaf mutes, and the insane have no legal standing in Jewish courts. Their statements are totally unacceptable in a court of law, both as litigants and as witnesses. See *Shev.* 42a, *B.K.* 106b, *B.B.* 155b. A notable exception where, according to some, they can appear as litigants is Maimonides, *Sekhirut* 2:7. See the comments of the Raavad, who disallows them from ever appearing as litigants.

†Pigeon-racing was a form of gambling in talmudic times.

Thus, even if two witnesses see two people enter a room and then, when the witnesses enter the same room, they find one man murdered and the other wielding a knife, they cannot be considered valid witnesses. A witness must witness the overt and explicit act in order to prosecute the case.

The requirement of two technically valid witnesses to the overt act, rather than only certain knowledge, is encumbered by many other technical requirements. Thus, the two witnesses must see each other as well as the commission of the crime.[3] Their testimony has complete credibility even if they did not see each other,[4] but it cannot be used to convict. Furthermore, if two valid witnesses were accompanied by an invalid witness, the testimony of the two valid witnesses cannot be used to convict.[5] The entire *hilkhot edut,* laws of testimony, is replete with details demonstrating that knowledge beyond the shadow of a reasonable doubt is not sufficient to convict. An elaborate theory underlies each of these requirements, but this does not detract from the fact that incontrovertible knowledge is insufficient.[6]

The Talmud tells us that the disqualification of various individuals from being admitted as witnesses is also based upon technical considerations rather than lack of credibility.[7] For example, the disqualification of relatives is a *gezerat ha-melekh,* a divine decree, i.e., a purely technical rule with no given reason. It is not based on lack of credibility. Maimonides paraphrases the Talmud:

> The disqualification of relatives by the Torah is not because they are presumed to love one another, for they cannot testify in favor of or against their relatives. It is simply a decree of the Torah. Therefore a friend or enemy is fit for testimony, even though they are disqualified to judge the case. The Torah has only declared regarding relatives.[8]

A similar technical disqualification applies to a variety of other potential witnesses. Some are disqualified for lack of credibility, others on purely technical grounds. A king is disqualified from being a witness.[9] David or Solomon, kings of Israel, could not testify. The Messiah will be disqualified from being a witness. The attitude of a court to a witness and the respect due a king are inconsistent.[10] Thus a king was not only relieved of the duty to appear in court as a witness, but was actually disqualified.[11] A woman, too, is disqualified from testifying.[12] However, Tosafot point out that this is completely technical and does not stem from a lack of credibility.

> There is no equation between the disqualification of women and the disqualification of slaves as witnesses. It is not a matter of credibility, but rather technical disqualification, as in the manner of relatives.[13]

Rashba (d. 1310) comments in a similar manner:

> Wherever the sages merely required ascertainment of truth, they did not distinguish between one witness and two. Thus, in a case of ascertaining whether a woman's husband is alive or dead, where we are concerned only with credibility, one accepts the testimony of all those who are technically disqualified, even one woman . . . is acceptable. For it is only where witnessed testimony is required that one requires two witnesses free from all technical disqualifications.[14]

Some disqualifications do carry an element of non-credibility. A person is incapable of testifying against himself. Maimonides points out that this is both a technicality and because of a lack of credibility.[15] One who has committed a crime is disqualified from testifying. Tosafot point out that this is sometimes technical and sometimes due to a lack of credibility.[16] Deaf mutes, the insane, and minors are disqualified because their statements are totally unacceptable in court, both as litigants and as witnesses.[17]

Slaves[18] and non-Jews[19] are disqualified technically because only a completely obligated Jew can testify. Lest this disqualification be equated with the disqualification of women, both Maimonides[20] and Tosafot[21] point out that the disqualification is for a different reason in each case. A woman is a completely obligated Jew.[22]

Credible statements, rather than witnessed testimony, are required in ritual matters. In this area, the statements of a man and a woman are equivalent. Thus, in determining the facts in any decision on Kashrut, family purity, etc., we rely equally on the statements of men and women.[23] Consequently, when a ritual matter has bearing on a criminal case, a woman's statement is accepted with regard to the ritual aspects of the case.[24] Thus, we have the following paradox. The eating of certain types of fat called *ḥelev* is a criminal act. The eating of other types of fat, called *shuman*, is not a criminal act. Thus, an accused person can be convicted if a woman testifies that the fat was *ḥelev* and two witnesses testify that he ate it. The logic is simple. For purposes of identification, all that is required is a credible statement and hence a woman's statement is accepted. For purposes of accusation, witnessed testimony is required and hence two witnesses, free from all technical disqualifications, are required.

There are times when two litigants come to court with insufficient evidence on either side. One of the valid means for assessing the facts, in many situations, is to administer an oath to one of the parties[25]—either the defendent or the plaintiff, depending on certain laws set down for the specific cases. Oaths are administered in court only to persons with credibility.[26] Oaths are not administered to gamblers, usurers, and pigeon-racers.[27] There are no oaths for slaves, mutes, insane persons, and minors, for they are not proper litigants and hence cannot appear as defendants or plaintiffs in the specified cases. Oaths are administered in court to men and women alike.

There are times, also, when a court is not bound by the strict rules of evidence and may employ credibility. Thus Maimonides says:

> A judge may decide monetary cases on the basis of things that impress him as true and he is totally convinced that the matter is so. In this case he may judge according to what he knows . . . even if the witness is *a woman. . . . as long as they have credibility with him* and the case impresses him as strong and correct, he may rely on it and judge . . . for the case is given over to the judge to determine what he considers to be a true judgment. If this is so, why did the Torah require two witnesses? For where two witnesses come in front of the judge, he may judge on their testimony, even though he does not know whether they testified truthfully or falsely.[28]

Maimonides quite clearly delineates the difference between credibility and witnessed testimony. Furthermore, he makes it quite clear that women are also credible.

Maimonides allowed a judge to decide whether to accept a woman's testimony in financial matters. The decision remains within the judge's discretion and cannot be challenged by any of the litigants. Rabbenu Gershom (d. 1040) and Rabbenu Tam (d. 1191?) went a step further. Their view is quoted by Rama.

> There are those who say that earlier generations have enacted that we accept the testimony of women in regard to those [financial] cases where male witnesses are not readily available. Such instances occur when a case arises regarding a matter in the woman's section of the synagogue or in other occasional matters where a woman chances to be present and there is no man. Consequently, some have written that even one woman is to be believed in cases of personal injury, etc. . . . The reason is that the plaintiff can not conveniently arrange to have male witnesses present.[29]

According to the Rama, in cases where male witnesses are not readily available, Rabbenu Gershom and Rabbenu Tam required the judge to rely on the statements of women. However, this does not mean that their statements are raised to the level of witnessed testimony; it only means that where witnessed testimony is not available, we rely on credibility. The practice of all contemporary rabbinic courts follows Rabbenu Gershom and Rabbenu Tam.

The question of why this technical disqualification was imposed upon women is completely open. It might be arbitrary or it might have certain deeper implications, as does, for instance, the disqualification of kings. In a secular legal system, there is no room for arbitrariness; not so in a divine one, as we explained earlier. The entire Jewish legal system is replete with *gezerot hakatuv,* decrees of the Torah. I am unaware of any authoritative or semi-authoritative statement regarding the possible involvement of implicit principles in the disqualification of women as witnesses. Hence, any search for such principles is highly speculative, and the following material is nothing but my own private speculation and should be regarded as only that. Furthermore, it should be emphasized that no matter what principle is adduced for this technical disqualification, such a principle remains outside the law. As we noted earlier in our discussion of the spirit of the law, implicit principles do not affect the law in any manner.[29a]

Ability to testify and obligation to testify are interdependent in Jewish law. Hence a king, who is excused from testifying, is disqualified. The reason for this is that a witness who can testify, and does not, violates at least one positive and one negative commandment—one requiring all witnesses to testify,[30] and the other forbidding a person to be a passive bystander while an evil is perpetrated.[31] Judaism does not grant anyone the right to stand idly by in the face of injustice.

This could possibly lie at the root of the technical disqualification of relatives. It is very difficult to imagine that the Torah would require a son to testify against the father. In addition, it is in the interests of Jewish law to protect the confidential nature of family relationships, much as the client relationship is protected in secular legal systems. The maintenance of an institution is very often more important than the needs of a specific case. The best way to grant a person freedom from compulsion to testify is to disallow all his statements. This is the most certain protection against illegal forced testimony.

To *require* all women to testify at all times might very possibly contradict their private role in Jewish life, which we discussed earlier. In a similar vein, the requirement that a litigant must appear himself in court, rather than appoint an attorney to appear in his stead, is waived for women because of the verse "The entire glory of the daughter of the king lies on the inside."[32] (It is interesting to note that in the United States, until recently, women could not be compelled to serve on juries. They always had the option of refusing jury duty. This is still true in most jurisdictions.) The technical disqualification of women in Jewish law may also be due to a feeling that it would be improper to subject women to the indignity of intense cross-examination in court. Hence, the reasons for the disqualification of women and kings would be similar.

There are many possible reasons for the technical disqualification of women, and no one really knows for sure. The only clear facts are that the ability to testify is neither a right nor a privilege, but an obligation from which women have been excused. The disqualification of women is a technical rule, rather than an expression of lack of credibility. Thus, women's statements are acceptable whenever credibility is required rather than witnessed testimony. Women's statements are not considered witnessed testimony. A woman's oath is acceptable in court, as is the oath of any credible person.

To equate the status of women in Jewish courts with the status of gamblers, usurers, and pigeon-racers, minors, deaf mutes, and fools, is to make the classic logical fallacy of "like result implies like cause." A cursory reading of Hume will convince anyone of the fallaciousness of such reasoning. Tom and

Dick both die. Tom had a heart attack. Therefore we conclude that Dick had a heart attack. Like result, i.e., Tom and Dick both die, implies like cause, i.e., they both had heart attacks.*

*While all agree that women cannot be witnesses, the Ritva and Rabbenu Tam say they can be judges in the manner of biblical Deborah (Judg. 4:4). Others agree, but limit a woman's ability to be a judge. Others say that Deborah was not a judge herself but guided the people and instructed and directed the judges. A teacher and religious guide of the people and of their leaders, yes—a witness or a judge, according to many, no.

14

Women and Contracts

Financially, a woman enjoys the same rights as a man, with the exception of certain rights in the law of inheritance, which will be discussed presently in detail. The Talmud says:

> R. Yehudah said in the name of Rav that the school of R. Yishmael taught of the verse "If either man or woman will commit any crime" [Num. 5:6] that the Torah equated men and women with respect to all culpable acts. The school of R. Elazar taught of the verse "And these are the [financial] laws that you shall place before them" [Exod. 21:1] that the Torah equated men and women with respect to all the financial laws of the Torah. The school of Ḥizkiyah and R. Yossi Haglili taught about the verse "and he killed a man or woman" [Exod. 21:28] that the Torah equated men and women as far as deaths are concerned.[1]

The Talmud explains that these verses are necessary because otherwise, since women do not generally engage in business, it might erroneously be thought that they were not granted full financial rights. To prevent any such misunderstanding, the Torah specifically informs us that women enjoy full financial rights. Only minors, fools, and deaf mutes have no legal standing.[2] A woman has legal standing totally equivalent to that of a man. She may enter into any contract she wishes (a right denied to her under common law), acquire and dispose of property (also denied to her under common law), be a litigant in all cases of contracts and damages—precisely in the same manner as a man. Certain seeming limitations arise because a woman, being generally homebound, usually leaves her financial affairs to her husband, but this represents practice rather than the norm and can be dispensed with by the woman within the framework of her Ketubah.

The institution of the Ketubah was designed to protect the woman. Upon marriage, a man becomes obligated to his wife on both a personal and a legal level—and these obligations can be enforced in a court of law. Certain extra laws were introduced to avoid abuses. A man is minimally obligated to provide for his wife's food and personal needs, clothing and household needs, medical payments, and burial; moreover, his wife will be supported from his estate after his death, provided not only food but general living expenses and home until such time as she may remarry, and supported her daughters, until they marry. There are also certain more technical benefits.[3] A woman was in fact doubly guaranteed. If she wished to be financially dependent on her husband, she was guaranteed in the manner just stated. If she wished to be financially independent, she could waive certain of the above benefits and be independent.[4] According to the Torah, a woman could go to work, keep her earnings, and still demand complete support from her husband. Such an uneven situation, where the woman contributed nothing to the household and received complete support, might well lead to serious marital tensions. Hence, the rabbis introduced a trade-off in marital duties. If a woman wanted to keep all her earnings, she had to reimburse her husband for her food, but the husband was still required to pay for her clothing, cosmetics, and personal needs. The Talmud is vague as to whether a woman who goes to work is still liable for a certain amount of housework.[5] Some scholars have obligated her in the payment of the entire household expense.[6] Others have exempted her from normal house-tending activities, such as child care, cooking, and washing.[7] These scholars have ruled that such duties become the husband's responsibility and expense. The practice in contemporary rabbinic courts is a compromise between the two positions.[8] A man cannot obligate his wife to pay the household expenses and must himself pay for the maintenance of a proper household and for child care, but a woman who has already paid for these out of her own money cannot demand reimbursement from her husband. On a smaller scale, there was a trade-off between various more technical benefits. But the decision between dependence and independence was left exclusively to the woman. She alone decided whether or not she wished to work and what she would do with her earnings.

During the medieval era, Jewish women often engaged in commercial activities. Many responsa of the period on problems involving women include the statement: "Nowadays, it is commonplace for women to engage in business."[9]

To say that women are not independent legal entities within the framework of Judaism, as certain feminist critics have done, is either to be abysmally ignorant of the Jewish legal tradition or to attempt deliberately to pervert it.

15

Inheritance by Women

The area of inheritance has often been cited by feminist critics as an area of serious discrimination against women. A careful and close examination will offer convincing evidence that the inheritance laws are one-sided—but in favor of women rather than against them.

Upon a man's death, a lien against his estate is created by the claims of his wife and daughters. A portion of the estate, sufficient to ensure the wife's support till her death, and the daughters' support until their marriage, is set aside. Furthermore, the wife and daughters are given usage of the home and household effects of the deceased. Thus, in practice, except for the very wealthy, the entire estate is frozen to be used by the wife and daughters. In fact, it was a common practice to have the widow manage the estate.[1] Any property that remains after the needs of wife and daughters are satisfied is subject to the laws of inheritance. It can be assigned by the owner to whomever he wishes—his sons, his daughters, or total strangers. Statutory inheritance is only applicable to a man who dies without having assigned his property during his lifetime.

To understand the laws of inheritance, a brief introduction to the theory of inheritance in secular legal systems will be helpful. The commonly held belief that it is a man's inherent and natural right to will his property to whomever he wishes has a very weak foundation.[2]

A will is a transferral of property after death and, as Blackstone noted, "The instant a man ceases to be, he ceases to have any dominion, else if he had a right to dispose of his acquisitions one moment beyond his life, he would also have a right to direct their disposal for a million years after him; which would be highly absurd and inconvenient."[3]

This is not only a theoretical statement but has many practical implications. The courts have frequently ruled that the Constitution does not guarantee the right of testation. In a seminal article, Bigelow maintains that even within the structure of Anglo-American law, "the title to property, subject to life ownership in a grantee, is in the State, and, but for the fact that the State has thought best to allow such grantee to designate the course of his property after death, it would always revert to the State upon the death of the grantee.[4] Intestate laws,* where the state disposes of the property of the deceased, seem to confirm this view. Since a man, according to this view, is allowed to will his property only because it serves the social good, the state can impose limits upon his ability to dispose of his property and even to disown his wife and heirs. While Bigelow's view may seem extreme, it does represent the logical foundation on which much of the current law of testation rests. The most serious limit on a man's right of testation is the demand of his widow. Under common law,

> the widow was entitled to a life interest in one third of the lands which her husband owned during coverture [the period of time that the woman is married]. She took this interest under the law and not by succession from him. It was not liable for his debts, nor could he deprive her of it by deed or will. . . . Dower [the above mentioned rights] extended only to real property. While the wife took an interest in intestate personalty [personal property other than real estate] under the Statute of Distribution, 1670, there was nothing to prevent the husband from giving away or bequeathing all of his personalty to others. Furthermore, his entire personalty was subject to his debts and the

*A person who dies without a will is said to die intestate.

> widow's share therein was computed only upon the net estate after payment of debts. . . . So far as [it goes] dower . . . [is] an excellent device for the protection of the surviving spouse. She is protected against the conveyance, the will and the debts of the other spouse. But there are a number of serious objections to the dower device particularly if it is the sole measure for the protection of the surviving spouse. While dower may have worked fairly well in the case of more fortunate families in agrarian society, it is not usually adequate in the present condition of urban living in which the average person owns nothing except personalty and perhaps a single residence. Even when the husband owns income-producing realty, a life interest in one third is often insufficient for his widow's support.* Then, too, the existence of dower impedes the realty transfer of real property, for the wife may be unwilling or unable on account of incompetency to join in the husband's conveyance. Furthermore, after dower has become consummate, the heirs of the land may be unable to find a purchaser who will pay a reasonable price, due to the uncertainties of the life duration of the doweress. In addition, the protection given against the debts may be unfair to the husband's creditors.[5]

The present structure of laws of estates varies radically from state to state. Virtually all jurisdictions have eliminated dower and introduced some modification. Most states "have guaranteed the surviving spouse an interest in both realty and personalty, similar to the alternative to dower provisions just mentioned, subject to debts and usually to inter vivos disposition by owner spouse. The trend of legislation is in this direction."[6] In this latter type, a wife becomes heir to one-third of her husband's estate and thereby loses her lien. An heir has no lien, for the obvious reason that to grant a lien to an heir would effectively eliminate all possibility of transferring property during one's lifetime. Thus, although a wife has advantages in

*The widow does not acquire the property itself, but only the right to use it during her lifetime. Hence, she cannot sell the property and dispose of the money.

being considered an heir, she also loses benefits in the presence of creditors and gifts during the lifetime of the decedent.

We turn now to inheritance in Jewish law. From a superficial point of view, there are no wills in Jewish law and hence everyone dies intestate—but this does not mean that a person cannot use other devices to assign his property. The legal problems outlined in our introduction are more serious in the Jewish legal system than in the Roman and Anglo-American. Not only can disposition be accomplished only by a living person,[7] but property can only be owned by a living human being. Thus, at death, property is completely removed not only from the control but also from the ownership of the deceased and passes immediately to the heir.[8] An heir other than a statutory heir can be designated by the deceased only by a deathbed gift, i.e., a gift causa mortis.[9] Jewish law recognizes a deathbed gift not as a gift but as the designation of an heir.[10] Thus, in effect, there are virtually no wills in Jewish law. However, there is an infinite variety of contrivances through which a person by means of a gift can transfer property to another, effective as of his death. This eliminates the necessity of a will and circumvents the lack of wills in halakhic jurisprudence. Some of these contrivances are revocable within the lifetime of the donor; others are not, depending on the nature of the contract involved.[11] It should be noted that an act of disposition by gift prior to death involves, of necessity, specific pieces of property rather than fractional shares of the total estate. Since assets remain stable when wealth is measured in terms of land, but not when it is measured in terms of personalty, this became a major problem when society began to shift more and more from an agrarian base. To circumvent the difficulty of assigning fractional portions of the estate, a practice arose wherein the donor obligated himself to pay a certain large amount to the donee. A conditional clause was inserted in the contract that upon receipt of a certain fractional share of the estate of the donor, the donee would renounce his claim upon the estate. This practice, which makes it possible for a donor to effectively will a portion of his estate to anyone he wishes, has become the standard way for a father to give a portion of his estate to his daughter.[12]

As mentioned earlier, the will per se cannot function in Jewish law for a combination of reasons. First and foremost, property can only be owned and disposed of by a living person. The subsequent use of the state as the guarantor of wills, which we find in Anglo-American law, cannot occur in Jewish law because no superagency is granted such extensive control and authority over property in the absence of any wrongdoing. The implicit assumption of Anglo-American inheritance law is that title to property ultimately rests with the state. In Jewish law, ultimate title to property rests with the owner. All property which belongs to a person at his death, and has not been distributed by gift, is immediately and automatically transferred to his heirs. If he has sons, they take the entire estate, share and share alike, with a firstborn son taking a double share.[13] If there are no sons, the daughters take the estate, share and share alike.[14] In the event that there are no descendants, a complex system of dividing the estate is used. The fact that daughters do not inherit if there are sons seems prima facie to be a gross inequity, but on deeper investigation it will be seen to be a great blessing.

The Ketubah was designed to strengthen the basic unit of Jewish life—the family. This was accomplished in two ways. First of all, the Ketubah renders divorce difficult by requiring a man to make a serious financial settlement with his wife in case of divorce.[15] Second, the Ketubah provides benefits to the wife and daughters after the husband's death, and these benefits far exceed the wildest imagination of anyone who has ever dealt with dower or its Anglo-American equivalents.

An heir has no lien on the property of the deceased for a variety of reasons, some theoretical and some practical. If A has a lien on B's property, this presupposes that A has certain rights to B's property. During a man's lifetime, the only rights to his property are held by himself and by others to whom he has specifically assigned those rights. Jewish law recognizes the additional category of *milveh haketubah baTorah* where certain noncontractual obligations are imposed by the Torah and whereby a lien is created.[16] An heir, though, has no rights whatsoever to the property of the decedent during his lifetime, and hence, for instance, the heir's renunciation of his own claims is ineffectual,[17] and he cannot negotiate his future inheritance. The inheritance is what the Halakhah calls a *davar shelo bah le'olam*—"rights which have not yet come into existence."[18] Thus, there is no basis for a lien. Furthermore, a lien by an heir would so completely limit the transferral of property in the lifetime of the deceased that for practical considerations it could not exist. Since an heir has no lien, he takes only what remains of the decedent's estate at the time of death. He thus cannot prevent gifts during the lifetime of the deceased and gets no share in these. Furthermore, his share is liable to all debts incurred by the decedent, which have a lien on the decedent's property.[19]

However, wife and daughter do not function as heirs but as creditors. Therefore they have a lien on all the decedent's property, be it real estate or personalty.* Their lien further extends to any real estate ever owned by the decedent subsequent to his marriage.[20] Neither gift nor sale cancels out the lien of the

*Originally, the Ketubah could be collected exclusively from real estate because a Ketubah, being a debt to be collected post-mortem, involved only a lien, and there is no lien on personalty. However, as society shifted from an agrarian base, the law was changed so that the Ketubah and other debts could be collected from personalty in the possession of the deceased at the time of his death. According to the Rosh, *B.K.* 1:19, this was done in talmudic times. According to most others, it was done in geonic times. However, Maimonides points out that if personalty is specifically mentioned in the Ketubah, as it is in ours today, then it always could have been collected from personalty. See Maimonides, *Ishut* 16:8.

Ketubah.† Since if two creditors with a lien attempt to collect, the one with the prior lien prevails, the wife precedes all creditors subsequent to her marriage.[21] Finally, since the wife and daughters have the status of creditors, their rights precede the rights of heirs.[22]

The exact rights granted in the Ketubah are as follows.[23] The wife has the option of a lump-sum settlement or continuing support from the estate of the deceased, including usage of the home and household effects of the deceased, food, clothing, medical payments, personal needs, and burial costs. The support terminates whenever the widow decides to take her lump-sum settlement instead, or if she remarries. The level of support is consistent with the standard of living of the deceased or the widow, whichever is greater. The lump-sum settlement is specified in the contract signed at the time of marriage, with a statutory minimum. The daughters are maintained from the estate and on reaching maturity are given a lump-sum settlement. The duration of the support and the nature of the lump-sum settlement vary with local custom and in accordance with the specifications in the Ketubah written at the time of marriage.[24]

The rights of the wife and daughters are those of creditors and hence create a lien. Thus we have the following Mishnah:

> One who dies and leaves sons and daughters, at the time that the estate is large, the sons inherit and the daughters are supported. If the estate is small, the daughters are supported and the sons go begging from door to door.[25]

The advantage to the daughters in being considered creditors rather than heirs is clear. They are guaranteed support before the claims of sons and creditors are satisfied. They precede sons because an heir does not have a lien, while daughters do. They precede all creditors subsequent to their mother's marriage

†This is true about all liens on real estate. They are not cancelled either by death, gift, or sale.

because they are prior creditors. Thus, while daughters do not receive an equivalent share in the inheritance of a large estate, since they receive only their support or a lump-sum settlement unless the deceased has assigned them his property, they are protected in the more crucial case of a small estate. The choice represents a realistic approach to the needs of women. The law recognizes that it is easier and preferable for men to go out and earn a living than for women.[26] Furthermore, a father can give his daughter by gift any portion of the estate he wishes. Since the sons have no lien, their rights of inheritance do not limit the father's ability to give a gift, and this may be the entire estate, excluding the widow's portion. On the other hand, the lien of the wife and the daughter limits the father's ability to transfer his property either to his sons or to strangers. The minimum claims of wife and daughter must always be satisfied first.

Each of the major practical problems with dower has been solved by the Halakhah in a different manner. The problem that arises when rental income from one-third of the real estate is insufficient for support is solved in a tripartite fashion. Originally, only real estate was liable to the claims of a Ketubah; as society ceased to have an agrarian base, however, the Ketubah could be collected from all real estate and personalty owned by the deceased at the time of his death, besides any real estate owned during the period of marriage. Furthermore, the entire estate is liable for the collection of the Ketubah, not the one-third of dower found in common law. Finally, the property of the deceased may be sold, if necessary, to provide funds for the collection of the Ketubah.

Thus, the maximum possible support is provided for the widow and daughters, at the expense of the heirs and also virtually all creditors of the deceased. While the Anglo-American legal system has been solicitous of creditors, the halakhic system has not allowed its own solicitousness to interfere with the rights of widows and daughters.[27] Furthermore, in a conflict between the widow and daughters, on the one hand, and the right of the heir to dispose of his property, on the other, the Halakhah has again decided in the favor of the widow and the daughters. The only exception to the strict policy with respect to the lien of the Ketubah was made in connection with support from real estate of the husband which has been sold. Here we find that the Mishnah says: "We do not remove property from a purchaser for the purpose of support of wife and daughters, for the smooth running of society."[28] As the Talmud points out, to do otherwise would so completely strangle the ability to dispose of property that it would render impossible any reasonable commerce. However, this was introduced only vis-a-vis the claims of support, but not vis-à-vis the lump-sum claims included in the Ketubah, which can be collected from any real estate owned by the deceased during the period of his marriage. All this indicates the lengths to which the Halakhah has gone in order to provide for the welfare of the wife and daughters in the structure of the inheritance laws and thereby to strengthen and maintain the integrity of the family as its primary concern.

According to Jewish law, a man may assign his estate by gift to whomever he wishes. The only restrictions on such gifts are the claims of his wife and daughters, which are guaranteed against all debtors and gifts. After the minimum demands of wife and daughter are satisfied, a man may assign his estate to whomever he wishes. The Talmud says that it is fitting and proper to grant sufficient gifts to one's children, especially to one's daughter.[29] However, if one does not choose to do so, he is free to dispose of his estate as he wishes.

Besides the practical benefits which we have described above, there are firm theoretical grounds on which the theory of inheritance rests. We read a strange tale in the biblical account of the laws of inheritance. Zelophehad ben Hepher had five daughters and no sons. When the land of Israel was being divided, his daughters approached Moses with the following claim: "Our father died in the wilderness, and he was not a member of the conspiracy of Korah, but died of his own sin and he left no sons. Why should the name of our father be deleted from among his family, for he did not leave a son? Give us an inheritance together with our father's brothers" (Num. 27:3). The request was granted. But how strange was the request of the daughters of Zelophehad! Why did they demand their father's rights rather than their own?

The explanation is straightforward and simple. One of the crucial distinctions between a free man and a slave is that the free man is given the opportunity to express himself through his work. A man's work becomes an extension of himself, and it is to this that he dedicates himself. When he dies, the person who takes over his estate also takes over this dedication. It is not just an inheritance of money, it is an inheritance of self. Money and other property can be assigned through gifts, but a lifetime dedication cannot be given as a gift—it must be taken over by an heir.

Thus, the Talmud says: "As far as inheritance goes, a son is preferable;[30] as far as *harvaḥa* [interpreted alternatively as "support" and "gifts"], a daughter is preferable."[31] Rabbenu Gershom interprets this as follows: "As far as inheritance goes, the son is given preference, for he is *kam taḥtav*, i.e., he replaces and takes over the functions of the father. As far as disposition of the estate by gift is concerned, a daughter is given preference and a larger share than the sons because she is not in a position to go out and earn a living, as it says: 'The entire glory of the daughter of the king is on the inside' [Ps. 45:14]. A son, on the other hand, can go and earn a living wherever and whenever he wants and is therefore given less." A daughter must be provided with the wherewithal of support, even at a son's expense, because a son is in a better position to support himself than a daughter. However, when it comes to inheritance of self, a son is in a better position than a daughter to effectively take over the father's function. That is why inheritance applies not only to property but also to such non-financial affairs as position in the community.[32] Thus, the Talmud says, unfortunate is the man who does not leave a son to inherit him for his work cannot be taken over.[33] There is no one to succeed him. True, in individual cases the daughters may be in a better position than the sons to take over the father's work, but the law must reflect the rule rather than the exception.

In summary, it is true that Jewish women do not inherit equally with Jewish men. The laws of inheritance reflect the real needs of both men and women. By denying women the status of heirs, they were guaranteed their support from small estates at the expense of the sons. The law recognizes that it is easier and preferable for men to support themselves than for women to do so. This right of the woman is guaranteed by an ironclad lien, something not granted to an heir. On the other hand, whatever is left over after provision is made for the support of wife and daughters can be disposed of by the deceased in the manner he sees fit. He may assign the rest of his property by gift to his sons, his daughters, or anyone else. The *Shulḥan Aruch* and *Naḥlat Shivah* contain all the legal forms necessary for the assignment of property to a daughter. Whatever is not assigned by gift is taken by the heir, i.e., the son. An heir is one who takes over the father's function; he is an inheritor not of money but of self. This was the complaint of the daughters of Zelophehad. Why should our father suffer? Let us take over his portion. The laws of inheritance are made primarily for the deceased, not for the living. The living have no right, per se, to the property of the deceased other than those the deceased himself assigns.

When the Jewish people entered the land of Israel, the land was divided into twelve sections. Each tribe, with the exception of Levi, was given a portion. These portions were subdivided among the individual families and then among the men over twenty. Women were not included in the division for a variety of reasons, both theoretical and practical. If a man of the tribe of Judah married a woman of the tribe of Benjamin and had a child, that child became a member of the tribe of Judah. To give women a portion of the land and at the same time allow intermarriage between the tribes[34] would have wreaked havoc with the entire tribal system. On the other hand, to prohibit intermarriage would have been suicidal for the Jewish people, for it would have split them into twelve separate peoples.

In addition, there are deeper theoretical grounds. Maimonides says: "Why did the tribe of Levi not acquire a share in the land of Israel with the other tribes? It is because Levi was designated to serve God and perform the Temple service and to teach God's law to the people."[35] The land was given to those whose basic task in life was to till the soil. The tribe of Levi was excluded; the earlier discussion explains why women were also excluded.

Let us now summarize our discussion of the financial position of women. The law attempted to find a middle path between two extremes. On the one hand, a woman's essential task is to be found in the building of a family and in the private sector of life. "The entire glory of the daughter of the king lies on the inside" underlies a significant body of halakhic and aggadic thinking. On the other hand, a woman should be given the opportunity, if she so wishes, to pursue her own financial affairs. The laws were set up to guarantee the possibility of the woman remaining within the privacy of the home environment, while at the same time allowing the woman who did not choose this path all the rights necessary for the pursuit of her choice.

16

The Marriage Contract

We shall now turn our attention to the area of marriage and divorce. In Jewish law, marriage and divorce are not sacraments, as in Christianity. They are viewed as contracts, and in many respects they are the paradigms on which all other contracts are patterned.[1] The Halakhah recognizes two types of contracts: the *kinyan issur*, a contract whose basic purpose is to effect a change in personal or ritual status, and the *kinyan mamon*, a contract whose basic purpose is to effect a monetary change.[2] The word *kinyan* has been totally misunderstood by many contemporary critics. It does not simply refer to financia ownership, but rather connotes a change in status. This change can be ritualistic, as is the case in many *mishnayot* in *Ma'ase Sheni*,[3] or financial, as in a variety of other cases.

Furthermore, the word *kinyan* has been used metaphorical ly in biblical and rabbinic writings to indicate the establishmen of a close and intimate relationship. Thus the Bible says: "Thi people that you have acquired [*kanitah*]" (Exod. 15:16), in dicating the establishment by God of His special relationshi with the Jewish people. The same is true throughout the Boo of Proverbs. *Pirkei Avot* says: "The Holy One, blessed be He has five *kinyanim* in this world: Torah, heaven and eart Abraham, the Jewish people, and the Temple."[4] This agai clearly utilizes the word *kinyan* in the sense of the establish ment of a deep and intimate bond.

The use of *kinyan* in reference to marriage combines bot meanings. Marriage establishes a close, intimate relationshi and is also a contract which results in a change of ritual statu i.e., it is a *kinyan issur* and not a *kinyan mamon*. True, many financial consequences and obligations result from the ritual change, but the purpose of the *kinyan* is merely to effect a ritual change. If this is not abundantly clear, a simple examination of the law of contracts will prove the point. If marriage were a *kinyan mamon* and the woman the acquired object, as some critics claim, she would write the contract in a case of marriage through contract, since in Jewish law the contract is written by the one who receives the money, not by the one who gives it—by the seller, never the purchaser. However, this is not the case with marriage, since it is the man who writes the contract.[5] Many other aspects of the marriage contract have also led the commentators to state explicitly that a wife is not the husband's property.[6]

This view contrasts sharply with the historic position of women in English law, where a woman was literally her husband's possession. Thus, until 1882 a woman could not enter a contract or even own property. Furthermore, until 1891 a husband had complete dominion over his wife, including the right to beat her and limit her freedom of movement.[7]

None of this is true in Jewish law, where a married woman may contract and own property. A husband was forbidden to restrict his wife's freedom of movement "for she is not in jail, where she may not come and go."[8] Not only was beating a wife frowned upon and forbidden, but it was a valid ground for divorce.[9]

The rules of contract are generally the same for both types of contract. This is derived by the *gezerah shavah "kiḥah, kiḥah misdei Ephron."*[10] Thus, although a purely ritual change is effected, money is the instrument of the contract. The essence of the *gezerah shavah* is that the formalism of financial contracts is utilized as the means of effecting ritual change.

Jewish contract law differs greatly from contract law in the United States. In American law, the execution of a contract is a bilateral act. Halakhic contracts, on the other hand, are unilaterally executed. A contract may require the consent of both parties, but it is executed by only one party. Thus, in selling a house, the seller himself draws up the contract, has it witnessed, and delivers it to the buyer.[11] The buyer plays only a passive role; i.e., he accepts the contract, and by so doing acquires title to the property and becomes obligated to pay the specified sum of money to the seller. Hence, to ask why the Jewish marriage contract is unilateral really misses the point, for there simply are no bilaterally executed contracts in Jewish law. Furthermore, while the act of acceptance is physically passive, it is a legally active role. The *kinyan* is finalized not by the simple act of giving the contract or of giving money, but by an act of acquisition on the part of the recipient. Holding the written contract, money, or ring for the purpose of effecting the *kinyan* is a legal act of acquisition which completes the *kinyan*. Legally, the recipient is active.

The only remaining question pertains to determining which party is the initiator of the contract in marriage. Since no contract in Jewish law is bilateral, this is really an either/or question. The Bible is most explicit on the subject: the man is the initiator of the contract.[12]

It may be that this choice was entirely arbitrary, as is often the case with certain kinds of laws where an either/or decision is required. For example, in the United States, the law requires traffic to keep to the right-hand side of the road, while in England traffic must keep to the left. Both choices are arbitrary since neither rule is intrinsically superior to the other.

At this point R. Shimon appears again. The Talmud says: "Why is it that the Torah gave the initiative to the man rather than to the woman? For it is the nature of a man to be active in the pursuit of a wife rather than for a woman to pursue a husband."[13] The Talmud adds that an unmarried man is more active than an unmarried woman in pursuit of a mate because he feels more incomplete. This basic emotion, continues R. Shimon, can be traced back to the story of creation, where woman was taken from man. Thus, when presented with an arbitrary, either/or choice, the Halakhah codified the man's basic emotional drive to marriage.[14] Man is driven to marry by his feeling of incompleteness more so than is a woman. From a personal and spiritual point of view, men need marriage more than do women.[15]

Is this part of R. Shimon's general theory rejected by the rabbis? Most commentators seem to think that R. Shimon's position is universally accepted in this matter. His position is rejected in other instances when he introduces the nonexplicit background of the law into the legal structure itself.[16] However, when he merely provides background to a law explicitly stated in the Bible, his position, they say, has not been rejected.[17] A few disagree and view the whole choice as arbitrary.

Divorce, like marriage, is a contract and hence unilateral. That the man is the initiator of the divorce contract is only one example of the equation between the contract of marriage and the contract of divorce that occurs continually throughout the laws of marriage and divorce. Marriage and divorce are typical contracts which are unilaterally executed.[18]

From a more practical point of view, divorce was rendered difficult to protect the woman.[19] Because of the Ketubah, a man who divorced his wife was burdened with a stiff payment (the statutory minimum is a lump sum equivalent to one year's support). However, this is not to say that a woman was always protected. Perverse people have a way of wreaking havoc with other people's lives. The Ketubah, in the hands of a perverse wife, can be a curse to the husband.[20] A man who cannot afford the payments of the Ketubah is burdened with his wife, come what may. Similarly, a perverse husband or wife can utilize the contractual nature of divorce to terrorize his partner by refusing to grant a divorce when one is in order. These are not the only cases where perverse people can ruin other people's lives, but they certainly are among the most agonizing.[21] As with all similar occurrences, it is the task of Jewish courts to deal with such perversities. In the case of an unwilling husband, the court can exercise all its power to force the granting of a divorce when it decides that one is in order.

While the man is the initiator of the contract of divorce, this does not mean that the woman is left completely at his mercy. There are many claims by a woman which constitute valid grounds for divorce. A woman may approach a beth-din with a claim against her husband. If the beth-din finds that her claim justifies her request for a divorce, it will order her husband to initiate the contract of divorce, and it can use all its power to force him to do so. Maimonides says:

> If one who is obligated by law to divorce his wife refuses to do so, a Jewish court at any place and at any time may beat him until he says: "I am willing." At this point, he may write the *get* [contract of divorce] and it is a valid contract.[22]

On the other hand, a woman may not initially approach a non-Jewish court to force her husband to grant her a Jewish divorce. However, if a beth-din orders a Jewish divorce and the non-Jewish court merely enforces the decision of the beth-din, the divorce is valid. Maimonides says:

> Similarly, if the non-Jewish court beat him and told him: "Do what the Jewish court instructs you," and the Jewish court pressured him through the non-Jewish court until he executed a Jewish divorce, it is a valid divorce. If the non-Jewish court, on its own, forced him to write the *get*, since one is required, it is valid according to Torah law, but was disqualified by rabbinic enactment [so that a woman would first approach the rabbinic court].[23]

Thus, it is no surprise that in Israel, where rabbinic courts are given recognition by the state, very few men manage to avoid granting divorces to their wives when ordered to do so.

In cases where they are able to avoid compliance with the court's order, it is because the State of Israel does not allow the full measure of coercion condoned by rabbinic courts. Rabbinic courts in Israel can order a man to be placed in jail for refusing to comply with their order, but Jewish law also allows corporal punishment to be enforced upon a man until he agrees to divorce his wife.[24] In the United States, the situation is far from ideal. True, it is only in unusual cases that rabbinic courts are ineffective in extracting divorces from unwilling husbands, but we must explore more effective techniques to deal with such instances. The imperative to fight injustice includes the duty of preventing abuses of the judicial system by the unscrupulous. However, when fighting abuses, care must be exercised not to destroy the entire system in the process. Contractual relations in general, and marital relations to an even greater degree, are intensely personal matters and can neither be created nor dispensed with except by the parties involved. The notion of a superagency that creates or dispenses with another person's personal status is entirely repulsive to the Jewish mind.

Much confusion has resulted from the misunderstanding of certain fundamental differences between Jewish law and the Anglo-American legal system. Some legal systems are state-oriented. Others are oriented to people and contracts. As was pointed out earlier, Anglo-American inheritance law is based on the assumption that the state is the ultimate owner of all property. Similarly, the state confers personal status, the state declares a couple man and wife, and the state terminates their marriage through divorce. Through adoption laws, the state can declare a man to be the father of a child to whom he otherwise bears no relation.

Jewish law, on the other hand, is contract-oriented. Each man is the owner of his own property. Furthermore, he is totally responsible for his own personal status. Marriage is a contract created by the willing consent of both parties and finalized by a simple *kinyan* in the presence of two witnesses.

Divorce is similarly accomplished by the parties involved in the presence of two witnesses.

17

Solutions to Problems of Agunah

The past century has seen various attempts to solve the problem presented by husbands refusing to grant divorces to their wives when a beth-din determines that one is in order. Unfortunately, the proposed solutions were made by persons not sufficiently versed in the Jewish marriage and divorce laws and thus were rejected by the rabbinate as being inconsistent with halakhic requirements.

On July 29, 1884, secular divorce was introduced in France. A short time subsequent to that date, a Rabbi Michael Weil of Paris declared that upon receipt of a secular divorce a Jewish woman would be automatically divorced from her husband in the eyes of Jewish law. He based this on a series of talmudic statements. Essentially he claimed that the contemporary rabbinate had the power to annul any marriage. Thus, he said, the rabbinate of Paris would annul all marriages terminated in secular courts.

The response of the rabbinic authorities to this proposal was immediate.[1] They asserted that while the power of annulment allows the rabbinate to introduce certain very limited changes in the marriage and divorce ceremonies, Jewish marriage can be terminated only by a Jewish divorce or by the death of one of the parties. Furthermore, the legislative prerogative granted to rabbinic authorities came to an end with the termination of the talmudic period. Among the many reasons the legislative prerogative came to a close is the fact that subsequent to the talmudic period no beth-din was universally accepted by all Jews, and universal acceptance is a sine qua non for legislation.[2] Hence, no legislative prerogative to change the basic marriage and divorce laws was granted to any rabbi or group of rabbis subsequent to the talmudic period; even in that period, no rabbi or group of rabbis was allowed to terminate a marriage other than by a Jewish divorce or on the death of one of the two parties.

This decision was accepted by the entire French rabbinate. Rabbi Weil, however, put forth another proposal. He suggested that all marriages henceforth be made conditional. Thus, during the marriage ceremony the groom would declare: "Behold you are wed to me. However, if the judges of the state shall divorce us and I not give you a Jewish divorce, this marriage will be retroactively invalid." Thus, upon refusal by the husband to grant a Jewish divorce, the marriage would be retroactively dissolved. The couple would never have been married in the eyes of Jewish law and hence no Jewish divorce would be required.

Rabbi Tzaddok HaKohen of Paris turned to Rabbi Isaac Elchanan Spector of Kovno, the leader of the European rabbinate, for his opinion. In a letter dated 4 Sivan 5753 (1893), R. Isaac Elchanan reiterated the initial opposition to annulment. He then proceeded to rule unequivocally against the proposed conditional marriage.

After Rabbi Tzaddok HaKohen passed away in 1906, the movement to make all marriages in France conditional was initiated again by Rabbi Joseph Lehman of Paris. Rabbi Yehudah Lubetsky, also of Paris, wrote a responsum detailing the reasoning behind R. Isaac Elchanan's position and called on the entire European rabbinate for support. When the European rabbinate unanimously opposed the proposed conditional marriage, the matter was dropped. The entire correspondence was subsequently published in Vilna in 1930 under the title *Ain Tnai bi'Nisuin* (There Are No Conditional Marriages). This volume contained responsa from Rabbi Chaim Ozer Grodzenski of Vilna, Rabbi David Friedman of Karlin, Rabbi David Zvi Hoffman of Berlin, Rabbi Shlomoh Breuer of

Frankfort, Rabbi Moshe Danishevsky of Slobodka, Rabbi Chaim Soloveichik of Brisk, Rabbi Meir Simḥah HaKohen of Dvinsk, Rabbi Yeḥiel Epstein-(the author of the *Arukh ha-Shulḥan*), Rabbi Menaḥem Krakowski, and a host of other rabbinic luminaries.

The opposition to the proposed conditional marriage revolved around the fundamental differences between financial and personal contracts. One can stipulate any condition he wishes in a financial contract, but marriage is a very unique type of contract. The underlying assumption behind a large part of Jewish law is that cohabitation is an unconditional act.

The etiquette required of Jewish marital relations demands that they express a complete, unconditional commitment by each party to the other. This translates into a contractual assumption that a couple that has lived together as man and wife has waived all conditions in their marital contract, and that the marriage cannot henceforth be revoked by a failure of either party to abide by the conditions of the contract. The few exceptions to this rule are so limited and well defined that they cannot be extended to cover the suggested conditional marriage. Since the entire scholarly rabbinic world subscribed to this thesis, the proposal was dropped, and most rabbis felt that the reasoning behind the opposition precluded any such method for solving the divorce problem.

The next proposal came in 1930, from the American Conservative rabbinate. Louis Epstein of Boston suggested that, subsequent to every marriage, the husband appoint his wife as an agent to execute a divorce on his behalf. Thus, if the husband disappeared or refused to grant a divorce, the wife, acting as his agent, would be enabled to execute a divorce on his behalf. The woman would, in effect, divorce herself.

The proposal was made in a book entitled *Hatza'ah Lemaan Takanat Agunot.* Epstein realized that such agency to execute a divorce presented serious problems. The thrust of his book lay in his attempt to demonstrate the halakhic propriety of such agency. In the book he called upon the world rabbinate to evaluate the merits of his idea. In 1935 the Rabbinical Assembly, the rabbinic body of Conservative Judaism, voted to accept Epstein's proposal .

Again, the world rabbinate responded with unanimous disapproval. At a meeting in New York, convened by the Agudat ha-Rabanim, various halakhic presentations were made, demonstrating the impossibility of the appointment of an agent in such manner to execute a divorce. Furthermore, it was pointed out, if a husband subsequently refused to grant his wife a divorce, he could simply dismiss her as his agent, and hence not only was Epstein's proposal halakhically unsound, but also of very little practical benefit.

A more serious objection was presented to the meeting by Rabbi Moshe Soloveichik of New York. His reasoning was similar to that of the earlier rejection of the Paris proposal of conditional marriages. Cohabitation is an unconditional act expressive of unconditional commitment. Thus the appointment of an agent for a divorce is nullified by cohabitation. Furthermore, any conditional divorce is nullified by cohabitation, and just as conditional marriages cannot be utilized, so too conditional divorces cannot be utilized. In his address Rabbi Soloveichik quoted the words of Maimonides:

> If he [the husband] was together with his wife after he appointed the scribe to write, or the witnesses to sign, or the agent to deliver the divorce to her, they may not proceed. It is logical to conclude this. A divorce which has already been delivered to her is rendered invalid when they are together, because we assume that they had marital relations [which invalidates all previous divorce proceedings]. Certainly a divorce which has not been written yet is rendered invalid. If the scribe wrote the divorce, the witnesses signed it, and the agent delivered it after they were together, the divorce is invalid.[3]

The effect of this law is to render impossible the initiation of any divorce proceeding at the time of marriage.

As a result of the unanimous protest by the world rabbinate, Epstein's proposal was shelved. The entire world-wide correspondence was published in 1937 in a volume entitled *Le'Dor Aḥaron.* In 1940, embittered by the rabbinate's rejection of his proposal, Epstein reiterated his suggestion in a book entitled *Le'Shaalat ha-Agunah.* Attempting to defend his position against his critics, he maintained that his method was a valid means of appointing an agent, but he completely ignored the complaint of Rabbi Moshe Soloveichik that marital relations render all previous divorce proceedings invalid. The book did not succeed in changing the minds of the rabbis whom Epstein wished to convince, and his proposal has never been revived.

In 1967 Dr. Eliezer Berkovits of Skokie, Illinois, published a book entitled *T'nai bi'Nisuin Ve'Get* (Conditional Marriages and Divorces) in which he asked the world rabbinate to reopen the question of conditional marriage. The book elicited virtually no response from the Orthodox rabbinate since his proposal was nothing more than a slight modification of the earlier Paris proposals. There was nothing substantially new in his book.

In response to a request from Rabbi Dov Katz, director of courts, Office of Religion of the State of Israel, Rabbi Menachem M. Kasher issued a responsum in *Noam.* After a detailed analysis of Berkovits's book, Rabbi Kasher concludes:

> In short, the author has not proposed anything new . . . to what was proposed in Paris, which proposals were unequivocally rejected by the rabbinic leaders.
>
> I have analyzed the work at length to show that in the essential point which is of practical significance in the proposed conditional marriage, he has clearly not proposed anything significant. He writes only of his doubts, his searching and seeking in the style of "for example, we might consider such and such."
>
> Even if he had advanced a brand-new type of conditional marriage, fundamentally different from the Paris proposal [which in fact he did not do] this would not alter the situation. The rabbinic leaders have rejected all conditional marriages and

> have decided that under no circumstances can one terminate a marriage without a divorce. . . .
>
> I am especially shocked that the author is completely oblivious to the fact that thirty years ago all rabbinic leaders of the day issued a decision, which was countersigned by over one thousand rabbis, in which they forbade and imposed a *herem* [decree of excommunication] against anyone who wishes to introduce the delivery of a get by means of an agent appointed at the time of the wedding. They included in this *ḥerem* also the proposal of conditional marriage. This fact is well known in America and was printed in the book entitled *Le-Dor Aḥaron*. Furthermore, Rabbi Yeḥiel Yaakov Weinberg, who wrote a letter of quasi-approval to Dr. Berkovits's book, has written to me as follows:
>
> "At the time that I wrote my letter, I was unaware of the discussion that had occurred in America. . . . Furthermore I am surprised that the author [i.e., Dr. Berkovits], who certainly knew of the entire correspondence in this matter, dragged me into this controversy. Because of my poor health, I am not capable now of dealing with a matter of such serious implications and I regret ever having written the letter to him."[4]

Dr. Berkovits's proposal was completely rejected by the Orthodox rabbinate. The Conservative rabbinate, faced with the utter impracticality of its own proposal of 1954, voted in 1968 to adopt Dr. Berkovits's proposal.

The various proposed solutions have placed the essence of the problem in sharp focus. In Judaism, marriage is a contract initiated and terminated only by the parties involved. No court was ever given the right to alter the marital status of a specific individual. The rabbis of the talmudic period were granted certain exceptional powers to establish or alter certain rules of the contract under the power of *afki'inhuh rabanan kiddushin minay*,[5] but these were universal rules of contract. The status of a specific person could not be determined by a court on an individual basis. A marriage, once finalized, could be terminated only by divorce or by death. Furthermore, the absolute seriousness of marital relations has ruled out the possibility of conditional marriage and divorce.

The only remedy that seems to be consistent with Jewish law is the one specifically suggested by the Talmud—the use of the secular judicial system. Outside Israel this means the enforcement by the secular courts of the directives of a rabbinic court—a beth-din.

In 1954 Professor Saul Lieberman proposed to the Rabbinical Assembly that the solution to the divorce problem lay in the Ketubah. He proposed the inclusion in the Ketubah of a statement wherein the husband and wife, at the time of marriage, would accept the authority of the religious court of the Rabbinical Assembly: "We authorize the Beth-din to impose such terms of compensation as it may see fit for failure to respond to its summons to carry out its decision." In this proposal, all aspects of conditional marriage and divorce are dropped. It was hoped that a financial penalty enforceable in the civil court would coerce unwilling husbands to grant to their wives religious divorces.

The response of the Orthodox rabbinate to this proposal was negative. There were a number of objections to Lieberman's proposal. The major one was that the contract wherein the husband or wife agreed to pay whatever compensation the beth-din would impose was halakhically questionable. A contract, according to the Halakhah, is required to be more specific. Most Orthodox scholars felt that such an indeterminate commitment as was proposed by the Conservative rabbinate was an *asmakhta*—a contract invalidated by the Halakhah because of its vagueness. Rabbi Norman Lamm of New York presented this view in an article in *Tradition:*

> The essential fault of the Conservative proposal . . . is its extremely indeterminate nature, a vagueness which Jewish law cannot tolerate as the proper basis for legal negotiation.[6]

Rabbi Binyomin Rabinowitz-Teumim of Jerusalem gave the same reason and also objected to this form of constraint to deliver a divorce.[7] Many forms of monetary constraint are valid, but certain forms of monetary constraint invalidate a divorce. The Ramah rules:

> When a man voluntarily accepted monetary sanctions upon himself should he refuse to issue a divorce, it is not considered an improper form of constraint, for he has the option of paying and not divorcing. However, there are some who invalidate the divorce in this manner. Therefore, initially one does not issue a divorce in this manner and our practice is to dismiss the threat of monetary sanctions.[8]

Rabbi Rabinowitz suggested utilizing such a contract but modifying it to avoid the problem of *asmakhta*—indeterminate contract—and adding the provision that financial constraint would only be applied if a competent Jewish court initially declared that the man is required to divorce his wife according to Jewish law. He advanced this as a tentative proposal and requested support from the American rabbinate.

This support was slow in coming for two reasons. First, in order to avoid the problem of *asmakhta,* the contract would have to be more specific and detailed. It was felt that once a contract was drawn up with specific and detailed financial penalties, the parties would be unwilling to sign it. In fact, it seems that this was the very reason for the vague wording of the contract proposed by the Rabbinical Assembly. Hence such specific contracts would not reasonably function toward solving the problem of enforcing a divorce where the husband is unwilling. The failure of the Conservative rabbinate to persuade people to sign their vaguely worded Ketubah subsequently confirmed this judgment.

Secondly, it is not at all clear whether such a contract would be upheld in the civil courts. This was argued very convincingly in a pamphlet by A. Leo Levin and Meyer Kramer, both of the University of Pennsylvania Law School.[9] They summarized their criticism of the proposal in

> the following major propositions: (1) the new *ketubah* in its truncated official English version is not a legally binding contract; (2) properly interpreted, the terms of the *ketubah* do not authorize the *Beth Din* to make an award for failure to give a *get*; (3) under arbitration law, authority of the *Beth Din* to make an award is, in any event, revocable; (4) punitive damages are not recoverable in a court of law and it will be for the court to determine whether the amount of an award constitutes a penalty; (5) in any event, court enforcement of a financial award made in order to compel the granting of a religious divorce would offend against the First and Fourteenth Amendments and would be unconstitutional.[10]

While these objections were made against the contract of the Rabbinical Assembly, the last three would seem to be applicable to any similar contract, including the proposal of Rabbi Rabinowitz.

I am unaware of any cases that have tested the validity of such contracts. Apparently, the agreement has not been used often enough to make it a meaningful solution. The fact that the Rabbinical Assembly accepted Berkovits's proposal in 1968 is the clearest indication that their own proposal had failed.[11]

The best way to effect a solution in the civil courts is not particularly clear. The small number of instances where a beth-din has been unable to extract a *get* has produced only a limited number of cases in the civil courts. Furthermore, great confusion has arisen regarding the details of Jewish divorce and the proper role of secular courts in their execution. Unfortunately, the courts have relied on less than expert advice in determining the halakhic facts.

The first significant case regarding Jewish divorce was *Koeppel* v. *Koeppel* in New York.[12] In the proceedings dissolving their marriage, Maureen and William Koeppel had signed an agreement containing the following provision:

> Upon the successful prosecution of the wife's action for the dissolution of her marriage, the Husband and Wife covenant and agree that he and she will, whenever called upon and if and whenever the same shall become necessary, appear before a Rabbi or Rabbinate selected and designated by whomever of the parties who shall first demand the same, and execute any and all papers and documents required by and necessary to effectuate a dissolution of their marriage in accordance with the ecclesiastical laws of the Faith and Church of said parties.

When the husband refused to authorize a *get,* the wife sued in civil court. The court ruled that forcing the husband to grant a *get* "would not interfere with his freedom of religion." The judge wrote:"Complying with his agreement would not compel the defendant to practice any religion, not even the Jewish faith to which he still admits adherence. . . . His appearance before the Rabbinate to answer questions and give evidence required by them to make a decision is not a profession of faith." The court seemed to assume that if the beth-din ordered a *get,* the husband would be required to authorize it.

Unfortunately, a case arose in 1973, also in New York, which complicated the issue.[13] Selma and Myron Margulies had agreed to "appear before a Rabbi to be designated for the purpose of a Jewish religious divorce." The court initially ordered Myron Margulies to appear before a beth-din. When he refused to do so, he was fined and jailed for contempt of court. The case was appealed and the decision reversed. The court, in its opinion, stated:

> It is argued that the court was without power to direct the defendant to participate in a religious divorce, as such is a matter of one's personal convictions, and is not subject to the Court's interference. We are told further that since a Jewish divorce can only be granted upon the representation that it is sought by the husband of his own free will, any such divorce, if obtained under compulsion by the court, would in any event be a nullity.[14]

The court, unfortunately, misunderstood the role of secular courts in enforcing a beth-din's order to grant a *get*. It also seems that the court misunderstood the entire process of Jewish divorce. Marriage and divorce are contracts in Judaism and require no declaration of dogma. The court, by comparing in its decision the granting of a *get* to Catholic confession, assumed incorrectly that a *get* is a sacrament.

Also in 1973, in *Pal* v. *Pal*, the court ordered the parties to submit to a beth-din. On June 17, 1974 the decision was reversed,[15] and the court, citing *Margulies* v. *Margulies*, ruled that it had no authority to convene a rabbinic court to decide whether or not a *get* was required. There was, however, an important dissenting opinion by Justice Martuscello. He pointed out that the court had erred in *Margulies* v. *Margulies* when it assumed that a divorce under constraint of a secular court is invalid. He further cited *Koeppel* v. *Koeppel* that an order to deliver a *get* is not a violation of constitutional rights.

At this time it is still unclear what direction the courts will take. There is precedent for the courts to refrain completely from forcing a husband to deliver a *get*. On the other hand, there is also precedent for a civil court to require a husband to appear before a beth-din and accede to its demand. However, it is essential that the courts understand the facts. A *get* delivered purely under coercion of a secular court is invalid. However, if the secular court merely coerces the husband into acceding to the beth-din's ruling, the *get* is valid. This is an indisputable fact of Jewish law. Also, it is essential that the courts realize that marriage and divorce in Judaism are contracts and not sacraments. It is certainly questionable whether forcing a person to execute a contract recognized as such only under religious law is constitutional. However, this is the only relevant question.

In the meantime, the standard practice of lawyers is to make the authorization of a *get* part of the property and support settlement. This is generally an effective means for dealing with husbands unwilling to grant, or wives unwilling to receive, a *get*. The legality of this practice was upheld in a recent case in New York, *Rubin* v. *Rubin*.[16] The couple had been divorced in Alabama, and the payment of support and alimony had been made dependent on the wife's appearing before a beth-din and accepting a *get*. The wife refused to accept a *get* and sued the husband for support. The court, in 1973, upheld the validity of the agreement whereby the husband withheld support pending the appearance of his ex-wife before a beth-din to accept a *get*. The implication of the decision was that it is completely legal to attach to the property and support settlement the requirement of giving and receiving a *get*.

A similar situation prevails in Canadian courts. Roberta Morris was divorced in Canada on July 14, 1972. When her husband refused to give her a *get*, she petitioned the court to force him to do so. She claimed that the ketubah is a valid contract, and that her husband, in her Ketubah, had agreed to act "in accordance with the law of Moses and Israel," which requires a husband to accede to the ruling of a beth-din. Thus the wife demanded that the court enforce her Ketubah and force her husband to give her a *get*. On March 16, 1973, Justice Wilson of Manitoba Queen's Bench ordered the husband to give a *get* to his ex-wife in accord with the demand of the beth-din, adding that where there is no conflict of dogma, the court cannot be said to be entering a religious dispute.[17]

On December 27, 1973, Justice Wilson's decision was reversed by the Manitoba Court of Appeals,[18] Chief Justice Freedman dissenting. In his opinion, which concurred with Justice Wilson's, he claimed that the Ketubah is a valid contract and hence the husband was contractually obligated to deliver a *get* to his wife.

Unfortunately, the justices who disagreed with Chief Justice Freedman misunderstood certain essential aspects of Jewish law. Some of them equated the Ketubah with a marriage vow, with its vague commitments to honor, love, and cherish the mate. This is incorrect. The Ketubah is not merely a marriage vow. Every party to a Jewish marriage, of necessity, must voluntarily accept upon himself all the detailed provisions of the Ketubah. Each of these obligations has detailed legal specifications and hence is not to be considered merely a vague promise.

Some of the judges wrongly assumed that Jewish law forbids the initiation of divorce proceedings by a woman, and therefore held that Roberta Morris, by initiating divorce proceedings in a Canadian court, had violated the tenets of Judaism. This is false. There are no religious directives whatsoever regarding divorce proceedings in a secular court. Moreover, a woman may petition a beth-din for a divorce. If the beth-din accepts her petition and orders the divorce, the husband must authorize the preparation of a *get* and deliver it to her. The beth-din can force him to carry out its directives if he refuses to do so voluntarily.

The case was appealed to the Supreme Court of Canada. The court's agreement to hear the case apparently indicated that it attached significance to both sides of the dispute, but the case was dropped because the plaintiff could not afford the additional legal costs attendant to a Supreme Court appeal. Thus in Canada, as in the United States, the issue remains unresolved.

Fortunately, cases where husbands refuse to grant divorces when required by Jewish law are few and far between, and a beth-din very often has sufficient power, by using social pressure, to secure compliance with its decision. Nonetheless, even if only a very few cases need to be resolved in the civil courts, we must do everything in our power to solve this problem. It is incumbent on the observant Jewish community to devise halakhically valid means of enforcing the orders of a beth-din through the civil courts.

18

Marital Life

Jewish tradition respects female sexuality and grants the rights of sexual fulfillment more to the woman than to the man. Judaism has always condemned celibacy and has none of the negative attitudes toward male-female relations so prevalent in Christian thought. Judaism's positive view of sexuality is reflected throughout the extensive body of Jewish literature on the topic, and one would suppose that only the most obtuse or biased person would fail to realize this. However, the feminist critique of Judaism has shown such a supposition to be naive. For instance, a few years ago an article appeared in the *Village Voice* which, in essence, claimed that Jewish men considered their wives ten rungs lower on the ladder than the lowest prostitute.[1] Others, more sophisticated and less gross, have perverted Judaism in a variety of other directions.[2] Judaism always suffers when Catholic doctrines are erroneously assigned to it. The fiction of the Judeo-Christian sex ethic has even convinced many Jews that Judaism shares Christianity's negative attitude toward sex in general and toward female fulfillment in particular. Nothing could be more mistaken.

At this point, it would be well to recall the words of R. Zerachiah Halevi, a twelfth-century scholar. One of his contemporaries, the Raavad (d. 1198), had written an account of the Jewish attitude toward marital relations entitled *Shaar ha-Kedushah*, or "Gates of Holiness." R. Zerachiah commented: "The 'Gates of Holiness' is entirely pleasing and beautiful, written with complete understanding, according to the faith of the devoted, to remove misguided actions, *but one does not give over matters of intimate privacy except to people sensitive in this direction*, as it says: 'and to the private will be granted wisdom.'"[3] Jewish thought on marital relations has always emphasized the absolute intimacy and privacy of this sphere of life. However, as R. Zerachiah warned, it is necessary to be sensitized in this direction in order to recognize the beauty of the Jewish approach. But there is another problem that prevents the Jewish attitude from being better known. Those who feel the absolute intimacy and privacy of this area of life are reluctant to discuss it in public, not because of any sense of guilt, but rather because of the private nature of the experience.

One of the most beautiful introductions to the Jewish attitude on marital relations is contained in the *Iggeret ha-Kodesh*, or "Holy Letter," ascribed to Naḥmanides:[4]

> Marital relations are holy, pure, and clean, when done in the correct manner, at the correct time, and with the correct attitude, and whoever says that they are something disgraceful and loathsome is gravely mistaken . . . and those who were influenced by Aristotle are mistaken.[5] For, underlying the philosophy of that Greek there is an element of heresy that is subtle and not easily felt. Had he believed in creation he could not have said this; for all believers in the Torah believe that the Almighty created all according to His great wisdom and did not create anything which was intrinsically disgraceful. For, if we say that marital relations are intrinsically evil and disgraceful, then so are the private parts of the human body, and if so, why did God create them? But God is pure of spirit and nothing comes from Him which is intrinsically evil, and He created man and woman and created all their organs.
>
> The matter is thus. For, just as the hands of a human being can write a Torah and can create the highest sanctity and at that time they are high and praiseworthy, and when they steal and murder they are evil and loathsome, so too is this area of life.[6]

The sexual area of human life is neither intrinsically evil nor intrinsically good. Man must endow it with these traits. At its highest, it is of the greatest purity and sanctity. At its lowest, it may be revolting and obnoxious. To express the essence of the Jewish idea simply, sexual relations are elevated only when they are expressive of a deep and permanent relation between a man and a woman. Because of the high degree of privacy and intimacy they entail, they reflect a unique relationship between the two persons concerned. Thus, sexual relations are condoned only within the marital framework, because marriage binds the two parties together and commits each to the other in the appropriate manner.

This is one of the reasons that Judaism insists on modesty in dress.[7] When a woman dresses in a come-hither, provocative manner, she uses sexuality as a means of attracting general attention, and eo ipso denies the intensely personal and private nature of this area of life. Husband and wife are reserved for each other, and the moment any aspect of the sphere of their private relations is exposed to public view, the intimate nature of their relationship is lessened.

Even within the marital framework, sexual relations are not permitted if either of the partners is not fully committed to the other. Thus, at the mere thought of a divorce, a man's wife is forbidden to him.[8] A couple who fought during the day are forbidden to each other that night,[9] for such a relationship would be purely physical rather than expressive of a deep love. The Raavad, in "Gates of Holiness" equates such a relationship with relations with a prostitute,[10] devoid of any expression of love and devotion, one human being merely using the other for his own selfish gratification. Any relationship of this type, even within marriage, is strictly forbidden. Similarly, relations are forbidden when either party is drunk or asleep, as not being expressive of mutual devotion. The examples are many, but the principle is straightforward and clear. The mutual devotion of each party to the other is the essential ingredient in raising marital relations to the level of sanctity and purity. At this level they provide a means of total communication of mutual devotion. As R. Menaḥem Recanti (d. ca. 1290) said: "Had relations been only physical, the Bible would not have referred to them by the term *yediah* [knowledge]."[11]

The Raavad points out that there are three motivations for a man in this area: (1) procreation, (2) the mitzvah of *onah,* (3) physical desire. The first two alone endow marital relations with sanctity and purity.[12]

The mitzvah of *onah* requires a man to maintain regular relations with his wife. Furthermore, the law established the husband's minimal obligation to his wife.

> The *onah* stated in the Torah is for each man according to his physical capabilities and his occupation. Men who are healthy and strong, who do not have an occupation that drains their strength, but eat and drink and stay at home, have their *onah* every night. Physical laborers, if they work in the city where they live, have their *onah* twice a week. If they work outside the city where they live, it is once a week. . . . People who learn Torah have an *onah* of once a week because the learning of Torah drains one's strength. . . . A woman can prevent her husband from leaving town on business so as not to miss her *onah.* So too, she may prevent him from changing jobs, which will lessen the frequency of her *onah.*[13]

In addition to regular relations (i.e., *onah*), a husband is required to have relations with his wife whenever she indicates a desire.[14] Furthermore, whenever he can anticipate her desire, he must have relations with her without her needing to indicate it to him. Such occasions would include the night that she goes to the mikvah and before he departs for a trip.[15]

In addition to establishing the minimum obligation, the mitzvah of *onah* requires a man to ensure his wife's satisfaction. The Talmud says: "A man is required to make his wife happy."[16] Since the requirement is *lesameah et ishto*—to make his wife happy—the mitzvah of *onah* imposes a requirement of tenderness upon the husband.[17]

Iggeret ha-Kodesh says:

> Therefore you should begin with words that will draw her heart to you and will settle her mind and will make her happy to unite your mind with her mind and your intention with her intention. Tell her things some of which will produce in her desire, attachment, love, willingness [and passion].[18] Tell her words which will draw her to fear of Heaven and to piety and modesty [*tzniut*].[19] Tell her of pious and modest women and of how they bore proper, fitting, and pure children. . . . You must not have relations with her against her will.[20] In such relations, because they are not done with great desire, love, and willingness, the Divine Presence does not rest; for your intents are different and the mind of your wife does not coincide with your mind. You must not fight with her or beat her in the matter of relations.[21] The Talmud says that just as a lion tears his food, eats, and has no shame, so too a man ignorant of Jewish tradition beats his wife, has relations with her, and has no shame.[22] It is fitting to draw her heart with words of charm and seduction and other proper things, so that the intent of both of you will be unified for the sake of Heaven. Similarly, one should not have relations while his wife is asleep for their minds will not be unified. Arouse her instead with pleasing words of desire as we have explained.
>
> In summary, when you are ready to have relations, ensure that your wife's mind agrees with yours. Do not hasten to arouse her desire, so that her mind will be at peace. Begin in a pleasing manner of love so that she will be satisfied first [the woman should achieve satisfaction before the man]. . . . You already know what was said about the pious man . . . who did not intend only for his own pleasure . . . but rather felt it as an obligation of *onah* and as a mitzvah in the Torah.[23]

A man is required to ensure his wife's satisfaction just as he is obligated in other religious demands.

However, this positive attitude toward marital relations was limited by a warning against overindulgence in sexual matters, just as one is cautioned against overindulgence in all pleasurable pursuits. The Talmud tells us: "The right hand should embrace and the left hand push away a wife, a child, and pursuit of pleasure."[24] The Raavad interprets this passage to mean that after a husband has satisfied the requirements of *onah* he must be guided by an attitude of moderation.[25] However, the husband's concern for moderation can never allow him to limit the rights due his wife as a result of *onah*.

Relations between husband and wife are the highest expression of *ḥesed*, overflowing lovingkindness. Judaism does not denigrate the physical, but the physical alone degrades man. It is through the union of the physical and spiritual, the union of body and soul, that man is uplifted. To be only body is to be an animal; to be only spirit is to be an angel; to fuse them together is to be a human being. Within the marital sphere, there are two aspects to the sexual drive: the physical and the psychological. These are present in both men and women. A man is required to maintain regular relations with his wife and satisfy her in both areas. This is the wife's absolute right. The Talmud describes special rewards for husbands who ensure their wives' satisfaction. A woman is entitled to complete satisfaction, and it is the husband's duty to provide it.[26]

On the other hand, if the husband asks, the wife must not refuse.[27] But neither may insist if the other is unwilling.[28] This does not mean, however, that one party is allowed to use marital relations as a means of achieving a specific end.[29] Thus Maimonides says:

> He may not have relations with her against her will, but with her will and out of talking and happiness. . . . Similarly the sages commanded the woman that she should not withhold herself from her husband in order to hurt him or to increase his love for her, but should listen to him whenever he wants.[30]

The Jewish concept of *onah* stands in marked contrast to the Western concept of marital duty, where it has always been the implicit assumption that marital relations are a husband's right and a wife's duty.[31] Jewish tradition insisted that it is a duty of both parties, but placed special emphasis on the husband's duty. The wife's duty to her husband is one of the responsibilities contractually assumed by both parties during the marriage. The husband's duty is an explicit command of the Torah and hence is not subject to prenuptial waiver.[32] Furthermore, many authorities are of the opinion that no waiver by a wife can ever cancel her husband's obligation.[33]

Marital relations are the highest expression of the intimate, deep, and personal relationship that can exist between man and woman. On this level, marital relations are raised to holiness and purity. To ensure this attitude, Judaism developed a comprehensive system of male-female etiquette. The motivating factor was not guilt or the intrinsic evil of sex, but the maintenance of sanctity and purity within the relationship.

The attitudes developed in the realm of marital relations are part of the total attitude toward marriage and life discussed earlier. The proper emotion of marriage is one of *hesed*, the mutual giving of each partner to the other. This is true in the area of marital relations as it is true in all other areas of life. To avoid the excesses which non-Jewish marriages have very often produced, and which form part of the legitimate complaint of the feminist movement, extra obligations were placed upon the man. While a similar attitude is expected from the wife, it is not a mitzvah. A woman's devotion to her husband is more natural and is part of the biblical curse to Eve:"And your yearning shall be toward your husband" (Gen. 3:15). A man is required to develop the same attitude through a specific mitzvah.

> We have been commanded that a groom be happy with his wife for one year, i.e., that he not leave the city for war or other matters, to stay without her for a long period of time. He must stay with her an entire year from the day of their marriage. Concerning this the Torah said: "And he shall be free for his wife one

> year and make happy the wife he has married" [Deut. 24:5]. The basis of this mitzvah is that God decided to create this world. His desire was that it be settled by fine human beings, born from men and women properly married,[34] for immorality is repulsive to Him. Therefore, He commanded the nation that He chose to be called by His name, that the husband stay with his wife, who is designated for him to raise a family, an entire year from the time he married her. The purpose of this command is that he become accustomed to her, that he deepen his desire for her, and that he internalize her image and actions so that he will forget the actions of other women. One seeks and loves that to which he is accustomed. As a result of this, a man will become distant from other women and will turn his mind toward his wife. His children will be proper, and the world will find favor in the eyes of God. . . . This commandment is applicable at all times and in all places, and one who stays away from his wife for many days, *even with her permission,* has violated this commandment.
>
> . . . There are some who say that with her permission it is permitted [for a long period of time].[35]

This commandment forms the basis of Jewish marriage. The curse "and he shall rule over you" (Gen. 3:15) was never interpreted to be a commandment.[36] Rather, the above commandment "to make his wife happy" was meant to curb the natural tendency implicit in the curse. The sin of Adam and Eve introduced tension into all relationships: husband and wife, man and animals, mother and children, man and the earth, man and his work. This was a curse—not a commandment, and certainly not a blessing.

Jewish marriage is characterized by mutual devotion. The rabbis made the general principles more explicit and somewhat more detailed. They demanded that each partner love and respect the other. However, in the final analysis, the details must be left to each couple and must vary with each situation. Only the broad general principles can be explicated.

It follows logically from the Jewish insistence on the strength of the marital bond and the fundamental role of marital relations in the establishment of this bond, that all nonmarital intercourse is forbidden. Maimonides says that nonmarital intercourse falls under the prohibition of "There shall not be any lewd men among the Jewish people; nor shall there be any lewd women among the Jewish people" (Deut. 23:18).[37] Naḥmanides disagrees with this derivation, maintaining that the prohibition is implicit in the injunction "And the earth shall not be filled with immorality" (Lev. 19:29).[38] Raavad, according to most authorities,[39] deduces it directly from the command to marry. Implicit in the command to marry, he claims, is a prohibition of all nonmarital intercourse. This is technically referred to as an *issur assei.* Most authorities seem to feel that Rashi (d. 1105) concurs with this view.[40] It seems clear that all authorities forbid nonmarital intercourse; the only dispute revolves about the source. The Talmud forbids a man from being in a closed or isolated place with any woman other than his wife, and hence it is clear that relations with a woman other than one's wife are forbidden.[41]

19

Taharat ha-Mishpaḥah

Combined with the laws governing marital relations are the laws of family purity—i.e., the laws dealing with the menstruating woman. Although unknown to the vast majority of Jews, they form one of the most fundamental areas of Jewish observance. The Raavad, whom we have quoted so often, says:

> And so that man should know that there is a God who rules over him, He has set for him laws and restrictions in his relationship with his wife, as He has set for him laws and restrictions in all other gifts that he has been given. If He has given man a field, He has commanded him on the plowing, the planting, and the reaping. If He has given him food, He has set restrictions and commanded him concerning eating. If He has given him clothing, He has commanded him also about its wearing. Even on man's body God set His sign with the covenant of circumcision. He has set limits on man's time by commanding him with the laws of the Sabbath and Holidays. Also, to the gift of marriage He has given commandments and has tested man and commanded him to separate from his wife at certain times.[1]

Jewish law functions to introduce the presence of God into all our everyday activities. Jewish man is confronted by God in every sphere—there is no area of life or action from which God is absent. Thus, the laws of family purity are not a primitive tribal taboo but an integral part of the system of Jewish law. Without these laws, a major area of life would be devoid of the Divine Presence.

Roughly, the law states that a man and wife are forbidden to each other during the woman's menstrual period and for a week thereafter.[2] At that time, after the woman has immersed herself in a special ritual bath called a mikvah, she and her husband are permitted to resume relations. Needless to say, these restrictions have a profound effect on married life. They function differently for different couples,[3] however, which may explain the diverse motifs that have been detected by scholars in the laws of family purity—the laws are universal but the response is individual.[4] In any case, for many couples these laws have been a source of periodic privacy. Some couples find that the periodic separation makes each spouse more dear to the other—they are forever looking forward to their mates with anticipation. For other couples, the laws serve to eliminate the monotony that often creeps into the marital relationship. Still others find that the laws enable them to develop powers of self-discipline that serve to elevate this area of life. When one is enslaved by his drives, it is very difficult to personalize them. If a man is to personalize his sex drive from womanhood, in general, to a specific woman in particular, he must be in full control of himself.

Through the personalization of the sex drive, the partner ceases to be a mere object and the sexual relationship becomes an expression of deep personal commitment. Furthermore, since the husband is required to relate to his wife for at least twelve days every month in an atmosphere that proscribes any sexual contact, he must learn to relate to her as a person and not as a means to his own gratification. Sex is dehumanized if the partner is viewed as nothing but a means to physical gratification who ceases to be of value when the physical end has been achieved. The laws of family purity humanize and elevate sex by enabling the partners to relate to each other as people rather than as sex objects.

The Talmud says:

> R. Meir used to say: "Why did the Torah say that a menstruating woman is forbidden for seven days to her

> husband? For, since the husband is accustomed to his wife, he may begin to find her unpleasing. Therefore the Torah said to let her be forbidden for seven days so that she will be as dear to him as the day of his marriage."[5]

In addition to their influence on the sexual relationship, the laws of niddah (the menstruating woman) have a significant impact on the personal aspect of marriage. Marriage is multifaceted; some of its elements tend to be overshadowed by sex and are never developed. Also, deep problems tend to be hidden until it is too late. Because of this, frank discussions are an essential ingredient in the building of a strong marriage. A couple afraid of the negative impact of such discussions on their sexual life may postpone them to the point where the underlying problems become insoluble. The laws of niddah provide a milieu free from the pressures of sexual anticipation. Deepening the nonsexual bonds, they reinforce the whole marital relationship, and in consequence the sexual bond itself is strengthened.[6]

The laws of niddah enrich the relationship between husband and wife. They were not meant to make women feel taboo or unclean. The Halakhah casts no aspersions on the physical state of menstruation, and surely a very bankrupt set of values is indicated if a woman feels she has lost her self-esteem when she cannot have marital relations for a week and a half. If anything, the laws of niddah make it possible for a woman to be valued as a person rather than as a mere sex object.[7] No knowledgeable Jew, for whom these laws are part of everyday life, has ever viewed them as a means of ostracizing women, condemning them, or destroying their self-esteem. On the contrary, every generation of Jews, each individual in his own way, has found that the laws of niddah add new dimensions to married life. But above all, the law of niddah injects the Divine Presence into a sphere where it can all too easily be forgotten, serving as a reminder that there is no area of life from which God is absent.

Needless to say, there are men and women who have not reacted positively to these prohibitions, experiencing them as nothing but an absolute expression of the divine will. In the area of family purity, as in other areas of Jewish life, observance is motivated by the simple fact that the laws express the divine will. However, since the laws are divine commands, the response to negative reactions must be education rather than abrogation. Much depends on the attitude and on the context of observance.

The medical aspect of family purity should also be mentioned. In an issue of *Israel Magazine*, Professor David M. Serr, director of the department of obstetrics and gynecology at the Sheba Medical Center, and associate professor of obstetrics and gynecology at the Tel-Aviv University Medical School, writes:

> On the whole, it is correct to say medically, socially, and hygienic-wise that the couple practicing family-purity ritual is healthier in some important aspects than the couple which does not practice this way of life. . . . It is undisputed statistically that Jewish women suffer less from cancer of the cervix, a rapidly fatal disease, than non-Jewish women. . . . Other possible medical complications of non-observance of family purity laws may involve infections of the male and female genitourinary tracts.[8]

Dr. Serr discusses the statistical information linking reduced cancer occurrence with the laws of family purity. He concludes that the link is a distinct possibility but has not been completely established. Other investigators have concluded that the statistical information is sufficient to establish the relationship "within the limitations imposed by the relative truth of scientific investigation."[9] All investigators agree that there are strong indications that the observance of the laws of family purity provides tangible medical benefits.

It remains to determine how all this interacts with the rationales for observance. No serious halakhic scholar has ever maintained that circumcision takes place on the eighth day because cancer of the male organ is unknown in males circumcised on the eighth day; or that Jewish women go to the mikvah on the twelfth day because women who have a standard twenty-eight-day menstrual cycle ovulate around that time; or that the laws of family purity are observed because they prevent cervical cancer and infections of the genito-urinary tract. These medical facts are striking, and some authors have attempted to use them as a basis for explaining the laws of circumcision and family purity, but the fallacy of their arguments lies in the connection of experience to logic. Jews observe these commands not for pragmatic reasons but in obedience to the divine word. The medical facts may well be an indication of some overriding divine plan, and one who views the Torah as God's word will stand awestruck at the coincidence of the laws of the Torah with the laws of nature. Beyond this, however, we cannot proceed.

20

Women and Prayer

Prayer is one of the central activities of a Jew's life. He begins his day with prayer and closes it with prayer, and most of his daily acts are accompanied by prayer.

Prayer in Judaism is termed *avodah shebalev,* the service of the soul.[1] It is an intensely personal experience in which the human being reveals his innermost concerns to God, as reflected in the words of the psalmist: "A prayer of an afflicted man, when he is troubled and pours out his prayer before God" (Ps. 102:1). For Jews, the paradigm of prayer is the biblical Hannah, a woman, of whom we read: "And Hannah talked [to God] of what was in her heart, only her lips moved and her voice was not heard" (1 Sam. 1:13). The private nature of prayer is guaranteed by its silence.[2] In all mitzvot where a person is required to say something, there is a principle called *shome'ah ke'oneh*—if one listens to someone else say the required statement, it is as if he himself said it.[3] Thus, all Jews are required to read the Megillah on the holiday of Purim, but one may discharge this responsibility by listening to someone else read it on his behalf. The Jerusalem Talmud[4] asserts that no such principle applies to prayer, because prayer is too personal to be done by proxy.[5] Every individual must pray for himself.

Women are obligated to pray as are men;[6] and their prayer is equally accepted by God. The Mishnah tells us: "Women . . . are exempt from the recitation of the Shema and from wearing tefillin, and are obligated in prayer, mezuzah, and grace after meals."[7] The talmudic analysis of this Mishnah has various textual variants, and hence there is some controversy as to its correct interpretation. The standard printed version reads:

> The reason they are obligated in prayer is that prayer is one's petition to God for mercy [and women also require mercy]. One might have maintained that since the verse in Psalms says one must pray evening, morning, and afternoon, we might consider it a time-bound positive commandment. Therefore, the Mishnah informs us that because of the aforementioned reason women are obligated anyway.[8]

Tosafot accepts this reading with a slight variation. The conclusion is clear. Women, like men, are obligated to pray daily. Since the special nature of prayer outweighs the fact that it is a time-bound positive commandment, there is no difference in obligation between men and women.

Rashi emends the text for certain technical reasons, but he concurs with Tosafot that men and women have the identical obligation in prayer. Both further agree that the obligation of daily prayer is of rabbinic origin.

The opposite view is taken by R. Yitzḥak Alfasi, and Maimonides. Their text reads:

> Women are obligated in prayer, mezuzah, and grace after meals, for these are positive commandments which are not time-bound. Women are obligated in all positive commandments which are not time-bound.[9]

Maimonides views prayer on two levels.[10] The Torah requires a person to pray at least once a day. Both the time and the text of this prayer are optional and may vary from individual to individual. The rabbis introduced a fixed text and also the obligation of praying at fixed times twice daily. When describing the obligation of Torah origin, Maimonides concludes:

> The number of prayers that one recites every day is not of Torah origin. The text of prayer is not of Torah origin. The setting of a definite time for prayer is not of Torah origin.

> Therefore, women are obligated in prayer, for it is a positive commandment which is not time-bound.[11]

Maimonides says that women and men have the same degree of obligation in the Torah's requirement of prayer, but he does not discuss the question of whether women are obligated in the rabbinic aspect of prayer, i.e., a fixed text recited twice daily. Most authorities believe that Maimonides agrees with Rashi and Tosafot that women and men are identically obligated in all aspects of prayer.[12]

While there are many interpretations of Maimonides' view, two explanations seem to be the most widely accepted. The first is that Maimonides accepts the reasoning of Rashi and Tosafot even though his text varies from theirs.[13] The second view is that the rabbinic expansion of the obligation of prayer applies to all who are included in the Torah's original command: since women are included in the Torah obligation of prayer, they are also included in its rabbinic expansion.[14]

The *Magen Avraham* is the first authority to suggest that there may be a distinction between the obligations of men and of women.[15] He is of the opinion that the obligations are identical,[16] but he notes that many observant women do not, in fact, pray twice daily. Apparently, he says, they must rely on some authority who assumed, with Maimonides, that prayer is of Torah origin. Furthermore, this authority must have assumed that women are only obligated in the aspect of prayer required by the Torah. The rabbinic aspect of prayer—i.e., a fixed text recited twice daily—is a time-bound positive commandment from which women are excused. This view would obligate women to recite a prayer every day, but not a fixed text at definite times. This view is not presented by the *Magen Avraham* as his own but rather as a justification for a practice which is prima facie in contradiction to the straightforward interpretation of the relevant talmudic passages.

Most subsequent authorities agree with the *Magen Avraham* that there is no solid support for the prevailing practice of women not to pray twice daily:[17] firstly, because Maimonides' view of prayer is not generally accepted,[18] and secondly, because it is not at all clear that even Maimonides would excuse women from the rabbinic aspect of prayer, i.e., a fixed text recited twice daily.

This discussion, however, only concerns the morning and afternoon prayers. The evening prayer, ma'ariv, was once considered optional.[19] However, since men have accepted ma'ariv as an obligation, it has become obligatory for them.[20] Women have not accepted ma'ariv as an obligation, and hence it is not obligatory for them.[21]

While the Mishnah specifically excludes women from the obligation of reciting the Shema, the *Shulḥan Arukh* says that women should be trained and encouraged to recite the Shema,[22] presumably twice daily.

However, in addition to the essential aspect of prayer, which is private, a public motif was introduced. This occurs in a dual way as *tefillah be'tzibbur,* prayer in public, and *tefillat ha-tzibbur,* prayer of the public. In *tefillah be'tzibbur,* prayer in public, prayer retains its essentially private nature. A collection of individuals, bound together by the common goal of their own unique, individual prayer experiences, pray simultaneously. Hence, a part of communal prayer is the individual recitation of the Amidah by each congregant. But since prayer is a communal as well as an individual experience, the *ḥazarat ha-shatz,* the hazan's repetition of the Amidah after the silent individual prayer, is offered on behalf of the community, i.e., as *tefillat ha-tzibbur.* True, it was originally introduced for the benefit of illiterates who could not pray for themselves, but once introduced it took on a totally different character. Since one person could not act as the proxy for another in prayer, a new form of prayer was introduced, a prayer recited on behalf of the entire community. All members of the community, whether or not they prayed individually, were required to participate in this additional communal prayer. For the illiterate this is the sole form of prayer, and it enables him to discharge his central duty of prayer. For the literate, while this form of prayer is required, individual prayer is also required, and the obligation of prayer is discharged only through both forms.[23]

The Talmud regards communal prayer as superior to individual prayer and hence more readily acceptable.

Maimonides, paraphrasing the Talmud, says:

> God always listens to the prayer of the community. Even if there are sinners among them, the Holy One, blessed be he, does not reject the prayer of the community. Therefore, one should associate himself with the community and not pray privately, whenever he has the opportunity to pray with the community.[24]

There is a crucial and critical difference, however, between the urgently preferable and the obligatory.[25] The Talmud does not explicitly discuss whether an individual is obligated to seek out a minyan and pray together with its members. This problem is addressed, though, by the medieval commentators. Rashi concludes from a statement in the Talmud that an individual is obliged to pray with a minyan.[26] Naḥmanides, taking his cue from another talmudic statement, disagrees.[27] If ten adult males are present, they must recite their prayers together in the prescribed manner, but an individual is not required to seek out a minyan.

Naḥmanides' reasoning is based upon an important distinction. Certain obligations fall upon individuals. For instance, every Jew is required to pray, whether or not a minyan is present. Similarly, the mitzvah of shofar is incumbent upon each individual. Other obligations are communal. This means that when a minyan—a community in miniature—is present, its members must act in a certain manner. Communal prayer is such an obligation, according to Naḥmanides. An individual has no obligation to seek out a minyan. However, when a minyan is present, its members are obligated to pray together—they may no longer act individually.

Naḥmanides introduces a third category which combines features of the individual and communal obligations: mitzvot which are individual obligations but can only be fulfilled in the presence of a minyan. For instance, the Talmud quotes the opinion of Rav Asi that one must hear the Megillah read on Purim together with a minyan.[28] Rav Asi maintains that the obligation of Megillah is individual but that a minyan is necessary for its proper performance.

According to all authorities, communal prayer is important and is more readily acceptable than individual prayer. Rashi views it as an individual obligation which can only be performed together with a minyan. Naḥmanides views it as a communal obligation and therefore rules that an individual should, but is not obligated to, pray with a minyan.

At this point, we must return to our earlier discussion. The inner dimension of striving is the essence of the Jewish heroic act, and woman was enjoined to develop this trait of personality to its highest degree. Thus, she was assigned the private role while man was assigned the public role. But in the Jewish view, as we discussed earlier in detail, to be hidden from public view does not imply inferiority. Lastly, let us recall the caution that was given earlier. Public and private are not exclusive categories but represent differing points of primary responsibility and initial emphasis. In woman one role is emphasized, in man the other, but both are present in each individual.

The unit for public prayer is the minyan, ten adult Jewish men.[29] While a woman may participate in public prayer, she cannot be one of the ten comprising the basic prayer unit. This is because women are enjoined to develop the area of private responsibility, and therefore always remain ten individuals rather than a unit of ten members. A minyan, however, is a public unit expressive of the public functioning of the community, and only men, as the public figures, can bind together to form a community.

The private nature of the directive of women has a second consequence. Since a woman has no obligation to participate in communal prayer, she need not seek out a minyan or pray with it if one is present. A woman is required to develop the inner and personal aspects of prayer. This differs from the obligation of a man, who is required to develop simultaneously both public and private aspects of prayer.

Women are not required to participate in public prayer and hence cannot lead public prayer. This is part of the general rule that only a person who is under obligation can perform a mitzvah for others who also are under obligation.[30] Thus, if one eats bread and is required to make a blessing, he can at the same time discharge someone else of his duty to make the blessing. But if one does not eat bread and hence is not commanded to make a blessing himself, he cannot discharge someone who is about to eat bread, and thus is commanded to make a blessing. Similarly, since women are not required to participate in communal prayer, they cannot act on behalf of the community in prayer. The duty of the ḥazan is to be the emissary of the community and act on its behalf. Woman, owing to her more private obligation, is not required to participate in communal prayer and therefore cannot act as the emissary of those who are.

Can ten women form their own minyan to recite the various prayers which require a minyan and to read the Torah? The answer seems to be straightforward, and the *Shulḥan Arukh* rules unequivocally: "We recite Kaddish only in the presence of ten free, adult, male Jews. The same rule is applicable to Kedushah and Borkhu."[31] As was pointed out above, ten women are ten individuals, not one group. The basis for the *Shulḥan Arukh*'s conclusion is quite clear. Although the Talmud does not explicitly discuss the formation of a minyan by women, it does discuss an associated but distinct issue—the formation by women of groups for the recitation of *zimun*, the addition to Grace After Meals, recited by a group of men. The

Talmud says that three women may recite the additional portion of the Grace After Meals which three men are required to recite.[32] The Talmud points out that the recitation of this addition requires three intelligent individuals so as to apply the biblical verse "Praise God with me and let us exalt His name together" (Ps. 34:4).[33] The grammatical form implies an individual addressing a plural, which implies a minimum of three. There is no requirement of a group, and hence women may recite this portion. Are women allowed to recite *Elokeinu*, the special addition to Grace required of a group of ten? Most scholars say no,[34] and their view is accepted by the *Shulḥan Arukh*.[35] The reason as expressed by the Vilna Gaon (d. 1797) is: "They cannot combine for anything that requires a minyan." However, even those scholars who do allow women to recite the special addition for ten would most probably not extend this permission very far;[36] certainly not as far as communal prayer or communal Torah reading.

There are two levels of praise of God which require the presence of ten. The highest form is called a *davar shebikedushah*.[37] Examples of this are the recitation of Kaddish, Kedushah, Borkhu, and the thirteen divine attributes. The requirement of ten is deduced in a rather complex fashion from the verse "And I shall be sanctified among the Jewish people" (Lev. 22:32).[38] However, there are forms of praise which, though not of the level of the above, still require ten. An example is the seven blessings recited for a bride and groom. The requirement is derived from the verse "In the congregations shall you praise the Lord God" (Ps. 68:27).[39]

The Talmud says that the reasoning behind the requirement for ten for *Elokeinu*, the special addition to the Grace, is totally different. The addition does not fit into any of the above categories. However, it is not fitting for less than ten people to refer to God as *Elokeinu*, "Our God." Those authorities who exclude women interpret this as saying that the phrase "Our God" can only be used by a community, not by individuals, and hence the criteria for reciting the addition to Grace are the same as the criteria for the first two categories.[40] While the reasoning of the authorities who claim that women may recite the additional sections is not altogether clear, they seem to say that even ten individuals can refer to God as "Our God" and the idea of community is not required. The *Mordechai* says this almost explicitly:[41] "Rabbenu Simḥah used to count a woman as part of the requisite ten, for even if men are obligated by the Torah and women only by rabbinic enactment, this is only relevant to the problem of a woman acting on behalf of a man. However, she certainly can be counted together for the recitation of 'Our God.'" Had these authorities felt that this idea could be extended to other instances where the idea of community is required, they certainly would not have been silent everywhere else. Only Rabbenu Simḥah, among the authorities who count women for a minyan in reciting Grace, mentions the possibility of a woman joining a minyan for prayer. He explicitly limits this, however, to the counting of one woman together with nine men. At most only one woman can be counted. Nowhere does any authority maintain that women can be counted for a minyan on the same footing as men. Discussion and argument as to the interpretation of their position is academic, however, since the opinion is not accepted. If women cannot combine to recite the additional part for Grace After Meals, they certainly cannot combine to say Kaddish, Kedushah, and Borkhu, and to read the Torah.

In recent literature, it has become accepted that women cannot be counted for a minyan because they are not obligated in public prayer,[42] and "a minyan is made up of ten people who share the same degree of obligation."[43]

The supposed support for this view is found in two instances where a woman is in fact counted for a minyan. Rabbenu Nissim (d. 1380), in discussing the opinion that a minyan is required for the Megillah, says that women may be counted.

"Is it possible that women can act on behalf of men and not be counted with them? Certainly, it is true that they may be counted."[44] The second instance is the one of martyrdom. The laws of martyrdom vary from instances of private martyrdom to instances of public martyrdom. One is required to martyr himself rather than privately violate the laws of murder, immorality, or idolatry.[45] One must martyr himself rather than publicly violate any commandment. The Talmud says that public means in the presence of ten Jews,[46] and Rabbi Yosef Engel (d. 1920) counts women in determining the number ten.

However, it seems to me impossible to generalize from these cases to other cases of minyan, even according to the very limited number of authorities who do count women in the above cases. Rabbenu Nissim's opinion about Megillah must be taken in the context of one of his earlier statements. He concurs with Naḥmanides' opinion that there is a fundamental difference between the requirement of a minyan for Megillah and other instances.[47] The obligation of reading the Megillah rests upon each individual. However, he says, the individual responsibility must be met in front of ten people so that one publicizes the miracle while he reads the Megillah. The miracle is publicized to men and women alike because both are equivalently obligated in the mitzvah of Megillah.

Rabbi Yosef Engel uses a similar logic in allowing women to be part of the minyan for martyrdom.[48] He says: "It is not true that the obligation of martyrdom is only in the presence of ten men. The Talmud's phrase is ten people, and a woman is also a person. The Talmud teaches us subsequently that we require Jews, but not male Jews. However, minors are excluded as they do not have the requisite intelligence."

Both these instances have a common strand. In both, we are faced with an individual who functions as an individual in front of a public audience. The requirement of ten is the definition of what constitutes a public audience. Women are included because they are intelligent adults who share obligation in the mitzvah under discussion.

The concept of minyan utilized in prayer and prayer-associated activity is different from the concept of minyan in Megillah and martyrdom. Here the minyan is a public unit whose unified functioning is expressive of the public functioning of the community. A minyan in this case is a community in miniature. The ten people bind together to form an *edah*. Here the reasoning of the Talmud in *Megillah* tells us that an *edah* is ten adult Jewish males.[49] As was mentioned earlier, it would seem that the reason ten women do not form a minyan is reflective of the private emphasis of their directive. Men are public figures and hence bind together to form a public unit. Women are more private and hence remain ten individuals.

Finally, it is impossible, if not totally circular, for Rabbenu Nissim to subscribe to the thesis ascribed to him. Following Naḥmanides, he is of the opinion that communal prayer is not an individual obligation but rather a communal one. This means, according to his view, that an individual does not have to seek out a minyan; rather, when a minyan is present, its members must recite their prayers together. To define a minyan in terms of obligation and then to define obligation in terms of a minyan is a circular procedure.

Thus, even if we would accept the opinion of Rabbenu Nissim or that of Rabbi Yosef Engel, which is shared by only a small minority of scholars, there does not seem to be any basis for extending this thesis to prayer or prayer-related activity.

Communal prayer has another aspect, that of communal Torah reading. The Torah is read in public on Monday, Thursday, the Sabbath, and all major and minor holidays. At each reading, several aliyot are distributed, the exact number depending on the requirements of the specific occasion. During an aliyah a man is called to the Torah and thereupon recites a blessing. A portion of the Torah is read, and a concluding blessing recited.

While our present Torah reading is of rabbinic rather than

of biblical origin, there is one public reading of the Torah of biblical origin—the *hakhel.* In Deuteronomy we read:

> And Moses commanded them saying: "At the end of seven years, at the appointed time of the sabbatical year, on the holiday of Sukkot, when all Jews come to the Temple, shall you read this Torah to the entire people of Israel. Assemble the people, men, women, and children, and the stranger in your gates so that you will understand and you will learn and you will fear God, your God" [Deut. 31:10–13].

As far as the biblical public reading of the Torah is concerned, there is no difference between men and women.

Whether or not women are required to listen to our present form of communal Torah reading is an open question. Most scholars say they are not. Others, including the *Magen Avraham,*[50] insist that as far as obligation to hear the Torah is concerned, there is no distinction between men and women. He cites, in support of his position, a passage from *Massekhet Soferim,*[51] a source of semi-talmudic authority.

Does this mean that women may have aliyot? We read in the Talmud: "All may be counted for the seven aliyot, even minors and even women, but women do not receive aliyot because of *kvod tzibbur.*"[52] This passage has been subject to a variety of interpretations, reflective of scholarly attitudes on issues other than merely the limited consideration of aliyot for women. Some have claimed that *kvod tzibbur* was the only consideration in mishnaic times, when not all the people who received aliyot recited the blessings.[53] Nowadays, however, women are excluded from aliyot for two reasons: because they cannot recite the blessings, and because of *kvod tzibbur.* Other scholars have said that women can receive some aliyot but not all seven.[54] However, most scholars have taken at its face value the talmudic statement that the only factor limiting aliyot by women is *kvod tzibbur.*[55]

What is *kvod tzibbur?* Unfortunately, not one of the

talmudic commentaries explains this phrase explicitly. It appears in a number of places in the Talmud with such a variety of meaning that proof by comparison is really pointless. Thus, any explanation must be speculative.

I believe that two basically different explanations can be found implicitly in the literature. One reflects the position of women in the synagogue. The other reflects the nature of the obligation of women as far as Torah learning in general and public Torah reading in specific are concerned. We turn now to the first explanation.

A person who is praying is required to concentrate only on his prayer. Anything which might tend to catch the eye or provide an alternative focus of attention is forbidden, as reflected, for instance, in the following law: "And in all places one should not hold tefillin in his hand or a Torah in his arm and pray because his mind is preoccupied with them. Nor should he hold objects or money in his hand,"[56] because this would also provide another focus of attention. When standing before God, one should concentrate exclusively on God.

In addition, a person who is praying is required to avoid anything that might make him feel self-conscious. Thus, praying in front of a mirror is forbidden. The essence of the prayer experience is total absorption. One must be able to lose himself totally in his prayer. Anything that causes distraction or self-consciousness eo ipso makes this concentration impossible.[57]

It is in this context that the first interpretation of *kvod tzibbur* lies. The sex drive is a very powerful and subtle aspect of the male personality. Sexual distraction is a consideration in many areas of the Halakhah, but most visibly in the area of prayer. Men and women are segregated during prayer for a variety of reasons,[58] one of which is sexual distraction. The presence of women provides the male with an alternative focus of attention, and also prevents him from attaining the feeling of solitude and intense concentration necessary for the deeper aspects of prayer. It is easy for a man to be oblivious to the people around him if they are men. It is more difficult, if not impossible, if they are women. The ability of women to catch a man's eye is known to every man, and oftentimes forgotten by women. The Jewish religious act requires inner drive and the inner experience. Both of these require the ability to divorce oneself from the people around him. The separation of the sexes was introduced as an aid toward this goal. The presence of women, of necessity, provides an alternative focus of concentration. In addition, men feel more self-conscious in the presence of women than in the presence of men alone. Just as external distractions from prayer must be eliminated, so must anything that increases self-consciousness. It is for this reason that R. Meir of Rothenburg says that women cannot receive aliyot but slaves can, even though neither group is obligated in public Torah reading.[59] Women distract, slaves don't! *Kvod tzibbur* reflects a sexual reality, not a legal difference between men and women.

It should be emphasized that this concern does not refer to adolescent sexual fantasies, although that factor cannot be denied, but rather to the ability of a male worshipper to divorce himself from his surrounding environment and from all other foci of concentration, a task more difficult in the presence of women than in the presence of men alone.

As a consequence of the above considerations, the recent innovation of removing the *meḥitzah* (the separation between men and women) during the Torah reading in certain avant-garde Orthodox synagogues seems to be precluded by *kvod tzibbur*. While the biblical prohibition of mixing the sexes applies only to prayer, the principle of *kvod tzibbur* tells us that distracting practices during the communal Torah reading are also forbidden. The underlying motif of the law applies here as well.

However, a group of authorities seems to interpret *kvod tzibbur* as reflecting women's lessened obligation in communal Torah reading.[60] If this is so, *kvod tzibbur* would disqualify not only women but also all who are not maximally obligated in the study of Torah. Women, according to this view, are not required to participate* in communal Torah reading because of their lessened obligation in Torah study.[61] Thus to take aliyot from men who are obligated to participate and give them to women is an infraction of *kvod tzibbur.*

Kvod tzibbur, as a halakhic concept, does not denigrate women, but rather reflects two fundamental Jewish attitudes. First, all distracting factors in the synagogue should be eliminated during prayer and prayer-related activities. Thus men and women are separated at all times, even during the communal Torah reading. Second, because of their lesser obligation in Torah study and communal prayer, women are not obligated in communal Torah reading. The aliyot remain with those who are obligated!

It is clear that aliyot for women are prohibited by Jewish law. Whatever the proper interpretation of *kavod hatzibbur* may be, the Talmud tells us: "The sages said that a woman may not have an aliyah because of *kvod tzibbur.*"[62] However, some imaginative Orthodox Jewish feminists have proposed what they consider to be a halakhically legitimate form of aliyot for women.

Part of the morning prayer, for men and women alike,[63] is the recitation of two blessings referred to as *birkot ha-Torah.* Through these blessings, a Jew expresses his gratitude to God for giving the Torah to the Jewish people and for commanding them to study the Torah. The second of these blessings is the blessing *asher baḥar banu*—"who has chosen us among the nations." Since this blessing is also recited by a man during an aliyah, feminists claim that it provides the means of giving a woman an aliyah that is not really an aliyah. A woman is not prohibited from delaying her recitation of *birkot ha-Torah.* Therefore, it is contended, a group of women can refrain from

*Obligated participation does not mean receiving an aliyah, but rather the obligation to attend the synagogue and listen to communal Torah reading.

reciting *birkot ha-Torah* early in the morning. Later they can take a Torah from the ark and read the portion of the day from it, and at that time, having not yet recited *birkot ha-Torah,* they may recite the blessing *asher baḥar banu* before reading each individual portion. Technically this would not be an aliyah and hence there would be no infraction of *kvod tzibbur.* However, since it resembles an aliyah, it seems to satisfy some contemporary feminists.

This practice has been opposed by all contemporary rabbinic authorities.[64] In my opinion, one need not look at the reasoning behind the suggestion to find flaws,[65] because the whole approach is fallacious. The *Hagahot Maimoniyot,* in the name of R. Meir of Rothenburg, ruled that activities that resemble a forbidden activity are forbidden.[66] To permit such activities would confuse people who do not understand the subtle differences between the permitted and forbidden activities. Something that looks, feels, and smells like a forbidden activity is forbidden. This ruling is cited by the *Beit Yoseph*[67] and quoted in the *Shulḥan Arukh.*[68] Furthermore, it is simple judicial common sense.

Something that looks like an aliyah for women will inevitably lead to aliyot for women. The subtle distinction between the recitation of *asher baḥar banu* on the one hand, which is supposedly technically permitted, and *borkhu* and the blessing *asher natan lanu,* which are forbidden, is lost on most people. Through the use of these supposedly technically correct aliyot for women, I have been told, the service at various women's conferences have had full aliyot for women, creating the fallacious impression that such aliyot are in full accordance with all the details of strict halakhic observance.

The Halakhah takes the view that one should not fool people or create the impression that he is doing something which he cannot in fact do. Women cannot have aliyot. Hence, the law states that it is forbidden to create a situation where they receive something that looks like an aliyah but is, in point of fact, not an aliyah.

An associated issue, although technically totally different, is the permissibility of women dancing in the synagogue with Torah scrolls during *hakafot* on Simḥat Torah. This practice has been opposed by all contemporary rabbinic authorities. My revered teacher, Rabbi Joseph B. Soloveitchik, told me that he opposed this practice when questioned by synagogues in Brookline, Massachusetts, and New York City. The basis for this ruling, he told me, is the Talmud in *Berakhot,* which says that just as there is an etiquette that regulates one's behavior when visiting someone else's home, so too there is a tradition that regulates behavior in the synagogue.[69] Thus, for example, eating in the synagogue is not permitted. An element of proper synagogue behavior, such as the prohibition of eating in the synagogue, is explicated in legal detail by the Talmud and by subsequent codes of Jewish law. The same applies to the introduction of innovations which our ancestors considered to be in conflict with the feeling of respect and awe owed to the synagogue. Proper synagogue behavior is determined by practice and tradition. Since it has been the age-old practice of synagogues that women do not dance with Torah scrolls during *hakafot,* the introduction of this practice would be a violation of synagogue etiquette.

21

Tefillin

The two mitzvot which traditionally have been restricted to men are the mitzvot of tallit and tefillin. The Talmud tells us: "Michal, the daughter of Saul, put on tefillin and the sages did not protest."[1] Tosafot points out that this is part of a larger passage to be found[2] in *Pesikta Rabati*[3] and the Talmud Yerushalmi.[4] The full quotation is:

> "And you shall teach it to your sons," but not to your daughters. He who is obligated to study is obligated to put on tefillin. Women, who are not obligated to study, are not required to put on tefillin.[5] [A question was raised: "But did not][6] Michal the daughter of Saul put on tefillin and the sages did not protest?"...R. Hizkiyahu in the name of R. Abahu said: "... the sages protested."

The initial opinion in this quotation, presented anonymously, is that women may put on tefillin.[7] The second opinion, presented in the name of R. Abahu, is that women are not allowed to put on tefillin. The Talmud quoted the anonymous opinion because it was germane to the specific discussion, but neither accepted nor rejected either opinion.

A variety of explanations of the controversy are given by the talmudic commentaries. However, the overwhelming majority offer the explanation first elaborated by the Raavad.[8] Tefillin are of the highest sanctity. There are detailed rules governing how tefillin must be treated and how to act while wearing them.

> One must touch the tefillin during the time that he wears them,

> for his mind must not deviate from them for even a moment. This is seen from the fact that their sanctity is greater than the sanctity of the *tzitz,*[9] since the *tzitz* had the name of God only once and the tefillin have the ineffable name of God twenty-one times on the head and an equivalent number on the arm. Tefillin require cleanliness of body.[10] Thus one may not pass any air while he is wearing tefillin. Thus one may not sleep or doze while wearing tefillin. . . . The sanctity of tefillin is very great. For while tefillin are upon a person's head and arm, he must be humble, God-fearing, and cannot be involved in laughter or idle talk, and cannot think evil thoughts. He must dedicate his mind to true and just matters.[11]

Hence, although the basic mitzvah of tefillin is that they be worn all day, only people of unusual sanctity, like the Vilna Gaon, did in fact do so. This is how most commentators[12] interpret the talmudic statement that "tefillin require a clean body, like Elisha Baal Kenafaim."[13] Only someone who is on that specific spiritual level may wear tefillin all day.[14] Men wear them, generally, only during prayer, the minimal period of time required. Similarly, although we begin training children to perform mitzvot far in advance of maturity, tefillin are not worn until shortly before bar-mitzvah. The optional wearing of tefillin is to be avoided![15]

Since there is no danger involved in the improper performance of most mitzvot, such as shofar, lulav, sukkah, and tzitzit, the Raavad asserts that women may perform all but three of the mitzvot from which they have been exempted. The three exceptions—tefillin, learning of Torah, and *semikhah** on a sacrifice—all involve possible desecration of sacred objects.

If *semikhah* is performed improperly, the result will be a violation of *meilah,* the laws governing the handling of sacred objects. The learning of Torah has many positive benefits, but there is also the danger of superficial learning. Improper treat-

*The ceremonial placing of the hands on the animal's head, when preparing it for sacrifice in the Temple.

ment of the tefillin violates the command to treat sacred objects in the prescribed manner, as described above.

Those who are obligated cannot be prevented from performing these three mitzvot, but the rabbis debated the propriety of their performance by anyone on an optional basis, weighing the positive results against the possible negative results. The debate in the Talmud on whether women may wear tefillin is concerned with this very point. Indeed, while the talmudic debates on whether women may wear tefillin, study Torah, or perform *semikhah* are independent, they all revolve around similar issues.

A small group of commentators have based their interpretation of the controversy on the Targum of Yonatan ben Uziel to the verse "No male garments shall be placed on a woman or female garments upon a man" (Deut. 22:5).[16] He interprets: "Tzitzit and tefillin, which are male garments, should not be placed on a woman."[17] The Torah prohibits the interchanging of clothes by men and women. This prohibition extends to certain activities which are viewed as distinctly masculine or distinctly feminine.[18] There is much discussion as to exactly which garments and functions are included in this prohibition. According to this group of commentators, the discussion in the Yerushalmi on whether or not women may wear tefillin really asks whether or not tefillin (and tzitzit) belong to the class of garments which is distinctly masculine. R. Abahu, who forbids the wearing of tefillin, follows the opinion of Targum Yonatan ben Uziel.

Some commentators view the controversy as an extension of the discussion of whether or not women may recite blessings on optional mitzvot.[19] Rashi views it as part of the general question whether or not women may intentionally perform those mitzvot from which they have been exempted.[20]

How is the controversy in the Yerushalmi resolved, and what is the practical outcome of our discussion? Maimonides and R. Yitzḥak Alfasi do not discuss the problem, and one might conclude from their silence that they are of the opinion that women may put on tefillin, but this is not conclusive. R. Aaron ha-Kohen of Lunel (early 14th cent.), in his work *Orḥot Ḥayim,* quotes Rashba (d. 1310) to the effect that women are allowed to put on tefillin.[21] Rabbenu Tam, as quoted by Tosafot, also rules that they may wear tefillin.[22] They disagree with R. Meir of Rothenburg (d. 1276).[23] R. Meir adopts the first interpretation of the controversy, namely, that the discussion in the Yerushalmi revolves around the optional wearing of tefillin. He concludes that the optional wearing of tefillin is prohibited and hence rules that women may not put on tefillin.

Naḥmanides, as mentioned above, concurs with his ruling, if not his logic. He is followed in this view by Tashbaẓ (d. 1444)[24] and the *Kol Bo* (14th cent.?).[25] R. Yosef Karo (d. 1575), in *Beit Yosef,*[26] quotes the *Kol Bo,* defending his view against that of the Rashba and apparently deciding in favor of the *Kol Bo.*[27] R. Shlomo Luria (d. 1573)[28] goes further than R. Meir of Rothenburg. He claims that the whole discussion in the Yerushalmi revolves around Michal, whose position was unique. Michal, a woman noted for her piety, wife of a king, and incapable of having children, was unique because her acceptance of the mitzvah of tefillin implied that she would wear them on an absolutely regular basis, without exception. Other women are not in a position to make such an absolute commitment, and thus, he claims, they were excluded from tefillin by all authorities. The Rama (d. 1572) and all subsequent authorities, following the opinion of R. Meir of Rothenburg, have decided that women may not wear tefillin. I know of no authority subsequent to the Rama who permits women to put on tefillin.

In conclusion, women are not permitted under any circumstances to wear tefillin. In view of the fact that the Rama, the authoritative codifier of law for Ashkenazic Jewry, and virtually all other authorities, forbid the wearing of tefillin by women, there is very little basis for a contemporary to permit the wearing of tefillin by women. The Rama follows the first interpretation of the problem and views the prohibition as rabbinic in origin. The optional wearing of tefillin is prohibited lest it lead to the desecration of their sanctity. This is a typical rabbinic enactment, and its purpose is the establishment of "a fence around the Torah"[29]; i.e., to ensure the proper performance of Torah-based laws. As is the case with all such rabbinic enactments, the law is binding on everyone, whether or not he feels that he needs the fence.

22

Tallit

The wearing of tzitzit and a tallit by women is a somewhat different problem from the wearing of teffilin. The authorities mentioned in the preceding chapter, who view the prohibition against wearing a man's garment as the source of the prohibition against the wearing of tefillin by women, extend their reasoning to the area of tzitzit and tallit. However, the overwhelming majority of authorities, whose reasoning is based on the sanctity of tefillin, do not extend their reasoning to tzitzit and approach the problem from a totally different perspective.

The mitzvah of tzitzit is not an absolute requirement, as are such mitzvot as tefillin, shofar, and matzoh. A man is not required to wear a four-cornered garment with tzitzit on them.[1] The mitzvah of tzitzit is optional. If a man never wears a four-cornered garment, he never incurs the duty of tzitzit. Only if he chooses to wear a four-cornered garment is the mitzvah of tzitzit incumbent upon him. Furthermore,

> clothing which requires tzitzit is exempt from tzitzit as long as it is not worn but is kept stored, for they are not an obligation of the tallit but of the man who wears them. Yet, though a man is not required to buy a tallit and wrap himself in it, so that he will perform a mitzvah of tzitzit, it is not fitting for a pious man to exempt himself from this mitzvah; rather, he should always strive to wrap himself in a garment which requires tzitzit, so that he will fulfill the commandment. At time of prayer he should make a greater effort. It is unbecoming to a great Torah scholar to pray when he is not wrapped in a tallit.[2]

Tallit is not a basic mitzvah. It is an act of extra piety which all men have accepted upon themselves. For a woman, the obligation is even more remote since she has the further option of wearing a four-cornered garment without even placing tzitzit on it.[3] Thus, for a woman it is a doubly optional mitzvah, and if a woman's sole purpose were to fulfill the divine command, she would only be motivated to wear a tallit if she were interested in the highest form of piety and regarded even the slightest mitzvah as having great significance. Therefore, according to the Rama, "If women wish they may wear a tallit and recite the blessing thereof as in other time-bound positive commandments. However, where it appears to be a case of false religious pride [*yoharah*][4], they should not do so, for even a man is not required to wear a tallit."[5]

The law of *yoharah,* acting in a way indicative of false religious pride, is commonly applicable to both men and women. The Mishnah says that a man is exempt from the mitzvah of Shema on his wedding night because his mind is preoccupied and hence he cannot concentrate on the Shema.[6] However, if he wishes to recite the Shema he may do so. R. Shimon ben Gamliel disagrees invoking the law of *yoharah:* "Not all those who wish to take the Divine Name may do so." Rashi explains the opinion of R. Shimon ben Gamliel in the following way: "If he is not known to the public as a very wise and pious man, it is nothing but conceit when he tries to show that he can truly concentrate."[7] Similarly, the *Shulḥan Arukh*[8] decides that it is an act of the highest piety for a man to wear two pairs of tefillin,[9] but that only a man of well-known and outstanding piety may do so. Rashi, followed by the *Shulḥan Arukh,* makes an additional and very crucial point. The decision whether or not a person has actually reached the highest form of observance and pious devotion is not up to the individual himself. It would be the height of arrogance to view oneself in such a light. Only a person who is known and accepted by the public as being very pious can act as if he were on such a level.

The rationale for the law of *yoharah* is clear. When a person who is not yet totally proficient in all that is required of him attempts to do that which is only expected of people on the highest level of piety, his motives are suspect. Had he been truly motivated to utilize his opportunities for complying with the divine command, he would certainly have made himself proficient in the most basic areas of religious observance first. The fact that he has not done so makes him suspect of religious exhibitionism and false pride.

The mitzvot are not meant to be tools for ego trips or for the advancement of a specific political movement. Judaism is very severe with those who use the mitzvot for their own personal ends. The law of *yoharah* warns us and limits us in this respect. The wearing of a tallit by a woman, a doubly optional activity, may be a mitzvah, but it is certainly a marginal one. A woman who is truly motivated by a desire to adhere to the divine command will first make herself absolutely proficient in more basic areas before moving into the more esoteric and optional ones. The value of mitzvot to a person should be determined by their intrinsic value rather than by their extrinsic appeal. Finally, it should be remembered that according to a group of authorities mentioned above, a woman's wearing of a tallit is an infraction of the biblical injunction against a woman's wearing a man's clothes.

PART III

Judaism, Self-Definition, and Liberation

23

Judaism, Self-Definition, and Liberation

Until now we have discussed specific details of the feminist critique of Judaism, but since the feminists address themselves to certain basic questions of self-definition, their views must also be discussed within a larger perspective.

Much of the feminist critique of Judaism is reminiscent of the famous story about four enlightened young Jewish men in mid-nineteenth-century Berlin. Faced by the many conflicts between their university education and the minimal Jewish training they had received, the four young men were ready to abandon Judaism altogether. However, since they realized that it would be unfair to reject Judaism without knowing its answers to their questions, they decided to send two of their number to Volozhin, the leading intellectual center of nineteenth-century Judaism. It was agreed that they would return at the end of two years to tell the others what they had learned. Two years later the pair returned. Their friends met them and asked about their experiences at Volozhin. "The two years were the happiest and most rewarding years of our lives." The young men who had remained in Berlin then asked: "Have you found the answers to our questions?" "What questions?" they replied.

The intellectual and axiological posture of the questioner is probably the most important factor in any critique of Judaism. Some questions remain questions no matter what posture is adopted. Others evaporate the moment the questioner changes his posture.

Furthermore, one's level of tolerance for problems and nuisances is very often dependent on the context within which he views them. One who faces a problem within an atmosphere that he finds deeply meaningful and rewarding will not be bothered as acutely by it as one who is basically out of sympathy with the specific milieu.

To indulge in a gross oversimplification, Judaism can be approached from either a religious or a cultural standpoint.* The approach of the religious Jew was outlined in the first section. He exults in the law, for it is his opportunity to fulfill the divine command. No mountain is too high, no obstacle too great, since his goal is to fulfill the divine will. Reasons and rationales are needed only for a deepened understanding of the divine will, not for motivation.

Not so simple is the path of the Jewish culturist. He follows the law because it is the culture of his people, but there is no uplifting dedication, no devotion. He is dedicated only to the cultural patterns and forms that have evolved over the millennia, and looks to rationales for justification.

The methodology of the culturist differs radically from the methodology of the religiously committed Jew. For the religiously committed Jew, there is no dichotomy between biblical and rabbinic Judaism. The oral law is *the* interpretation of the written law. Biblical and rabbinic Judaism are elements of one unit, and explanations for biblical laws are sought in the rabbinic writings. The study of other ancient cultures may be interesting, but it provides no real insight into the true meaning of the divine will. The culturist sees a complete dichotomy between biblical and rabbinic Judaism. They are different stages in an evolving culture. According to this view, a proper understanding of Judaism cannot be gleaned solely from internal sources; it is also necessary to determine how Judaism evolved from its neighboring cultures. Thus Judaism loses its

*Most approaches to Judaism represent a combination of elements of both of these approaches.

uniqueness and must be viewed as just another culture in the perspective of sister and parent cultures.

While even the religiously committed Jew recognizes the existence of similarities between Judaism and other religions, his basic approach is the one outlined by Maimonides. By his own admission, Maimonides was an ardent scholar of comparative religions.[1] However, in *Iggeret Taiman* he says:

> The difference between our religion and those that are similar to it is the difference between a live man who thinks and a statue artfully created from marble, wood, silver, or gold in the form of a man. The fool, in the knowledge of God and in God's work, when he sees a statue similar to a man in outer form, structure, size, and color, will think that the two are identical because he sees that superficially one is like the other. However, the wise man, who understands the inner workings of things, knows that on the inside of the statue there is no handiwork and that the inside working of the human being is truly wondrous. . . . so the foolish and ignorant person, when he approaches our Torah and the words of the prophets, and when he compares our Torah to foreign religions, will think there is a comparison between them. He will find in the Torah of God things which are forbidden and things which are permitted. In both he will find rituals, and both forbid, promise reward, and threaten punishment. However, had he understood the hidden things of both, he would find that the divinely given Torah has great wisdom in its workings . . . and that those similar cultures lack real content, but have only superficial form and should seem as ridiculous as does a monkey who tries to imitate a human being.[2]

The religiously committed Jew does not deny the existence of similarities between religions, but he sees beyond them to the grandeur and depth which have allowed the Torah alone to survive over the millennia.

This methodological posture affects not only the investigation of the origins of Jewish practice and law, but also the proper response to the axiological and cultural challenges of modern life. If one adopts the posture of the culturist, he is burdened with a serious, if not impossible, task. Somehow, he must find a middle path which is indelibly stamped with Jewish culture but which does not reject the cultural norms of contemporary life. This represents, to him, part of the age-old process of assimilating into the current of Jewish life the cultural norms and forms of sister cultures—which he sees as the essential character of Jewish cultural history.

Not so is the path of the religiously committed Jew. To him, Judaism represents the eternal counterculture, which at times takes the outer garb of sister cultures but can never dare assimilate their values and mores. For to do so would verily be a total sacrilege, a denial of the divine directive *le'taken olam bemalkhut sh'*—to remake the world into a divine kingdom, to show the world the total uniqueness of the divine message. Judaism does not assimilate contemporary values, for to do so would be to implicitly reject the divine imperative as the source of all value.

At this point, a question presents itself: What has guaranteed the intactness of Jewish law and prevented it from incorporating the cultural biases and values of the cultures in which it has flourished? The answer lies in two places—in the structure of Jewish law, and in the psychology of the men who have been active in its development.

In discussing the structure of Jewish law, it is necessary to distinguish between various levels. First, there is the written law—those laws and ordinances specifically mentioned in the written text of the Torah. Second, there is the oral law given to Moses on Sinai and passed on from generation to generation. The oral law is to be viewed on three levels.[3] There are, to begin with, specific laws, many of which have no mention in the written law, called *halakhot le'Moshe mi'Sinai* הלכות למשה מסיני. Secondly, there are specific interpretations of biblical passages, referred to as *perushim ha-mekubalim mi'Moshe mi'Sinai*

פירושים המקובלים ממשה מסיני. Finally, the largest part of the corpus of the oral law is based upon the use of various technical rules—also given at Sinai—to interpret the written law. A halakhic argument is correct or incorrect depending upon its adherence to the technical rules—it cannot be rejected simply because its conclusions are undesirable.

This absolute adherence to the technical aspect of argumentation may seem overly restrictive to the uninitiated, but it has allowed Judaism to define itself as a unified counterculture within a medley of other cultures. Jewish scholars from different regions and societies can debate points with each other because of this adherence to technical rules. This is true in the post-talmudic period as well as the tannaitic and amoraic periods. Although the technical rules changed with the closing of the Talmud, Jewish law still remains a technical field. Since all legal arguments must measure up to the same technical standards, and stand or fall depending on that, the law was prevented from fracturing into separate laws, each dominated by a different cultural bias. Maimonides could correspond with halakhic scholars in Lunel and Baghdad. All three lived in widely divergent cultural frameworks, but the technical nature of halakhic discourse maintained the unity necessary for their discussion. This is not to say that certain specific ideas are not found only in the Spanish school, or only in the French school, etc., but this is due largely to the dominating influence of certain individuals rather than to a cultural bias. The basic underlying unity of halakhic discourse has allowed the Halakhah to maintain its unity, and as a result, today, three thousand years after Sinai, there is essentially only one law. Had each generation and each region incorporated its local cultural bias and axiology into Jewish law, there would now be a multitude of laws with very little area of common discourse between them.

The integrity of halakhic argumentation is further ensured by two characteristics that typify all serious interpreters of the law. Because they see themselves as working with divine law, they know that the stakes are too high to allow any course but brutal honesty. This is exemplified in the comment of Naḥmanides to the verse "for the law belongs to God" (Deut. 1:17): "And He has placed us in His stead, and if one is dishonest, he has violated his position as a divine messenger." Fully aware that he is dealing with divine law, the interpreter of the law knows that the most significant and crucial consequences may ride upon his halakhic decision, and therefore he will insist on arriving at the correct interpretation in accordance with the technical rules. It is not for him to introduce his own ideas, but only through his reasoning to perceive and interpret the divine message. Anyone who takes this responsibility seriously cannot but make the most strenuous effort to maintain the purity of his technical reasoning.

It is at this juncture that the second consideration enters. A Jew who takes the divine directive with the utmost seriousness and also lives in another culture can never lead an authentically bicultural existence. He may speak the language and have the intellectual veneer of the other culture, he may be totally conversant with its ways and values, but if he takes the divine directive seriously, he is but a visitor in the other culture, and Judaism remains his cultural home. This is not an ideal but a fact of life—an immediate consequence of the overwhelming nature of the divine directive. These two factors maintain the integrity of Jewish values. They keep the technical arguments of halakhic discourse free of any cultural bias, and in this way they have preserved Judaism as a counterculture throughout its history.

So it is that a religiously committed Jew must confront all current axiological and cultural challenges from the unique perspective of the Torah—allowing his value judgments to be determined by the source of all value, the divine word. Values may not be assimilated, for to do so would be an implicit rejection of the divine imperative as the source of all value.

The feminist critique of Judaism has proceeded on a dual basis—first of all, on the level of specific laws, and second, on the level of role definition and areas and directions for self-fulfillment. On the first level, as was pointed out above, the assimilation of current axiological tendencies into the structure of Jewish law cannot be permitted under any circumstances. To change laws because of a shift in values is absolutely out of the question. The only area where limited accommodation is possible is the financial, where a large amount of accommodation has already taken place. In the financial area, contemporary Jewish courts are given wide legislative powers and prerogatives. Certain aspects of financial protection for women implicit in the marriage laws demand a recognition of the prevailing economic conditions of the day. In Israel, where rabbinic courts have been granted significant powers by the government, many *takkanot*—new practices—have been introduced and are enforced. These are largely unknown in the United States, where most Jews, unfortunately, do not bind themselves by the financial decisions of rabbinic courts. Under current circumstances, financial legislation by rabbinic courts would be a meaningless gesture.

As far as the larger and more significant issue of role definition is concerned, the answer, like the problem, must be presented in more general terms. No one ever seeks self-definition without restrictions. Sometimes the restictions may be self-imposed, but generally they are the restrictions of the cultural-axiological framework within which self-definition is sought. Nearly everyone falls into the latter category. Only a Robinson Crusoe would have the opportunity to define himself without an external structure. However, even such a person would eventually need to fall back on the framework of his background. Any framework within which one defines himself is eo ipso restrictive. Of course, if the values and cultural bias of that framework are accepted, these restrictions are either not felt at all or else certainly not in any acute sense. Thus, when discussing the problem, as raised by the Jewish women's movement, of self-definition for women we must examine the cultural biases that underlie the critique.

The Hebrew word for "definition," *hagdarah,* comes from the root *geder,* meaning "fence." The word *define* in English connotes a similar idea and comes from the same basic concept. The reason for this is clear. Definition is a limiting process. Self-definition is a very limiting process. It states that which differentiates one from others. Jewish self-definition is in reality self-transcendence. It shows how to transcend the finitude of human existence and reach out to the ultimate. The Jewish concept of free choice says that man is free to choose the path of self-transcendence. If, for various psychological, cultural, or other motivational reasons, he feels that his path is not the path of self-transcendence, the fault lies within himself, but he is free to change, because a person is given the free choice to mold himself. There is no rigid, unalterable self which awaits discovery,[4] but rather a highly malleable human being and a free will, which together should seek value and meaning.

The Torah says: "And God created man in his image, in the image of God did He create him" (Gen. 1:27). Rashi, commenting on the first phrase, says that the first image does not refer to the image of God but to man's own image. Man was created with certain talents, drives, and predilections, and was given the wherewithal to develop them. But this does not mean that he may single-mindedly pursue *all* of them. The geonim[5] (Babylonian scholars from the 6th through the 11th cent.) interpret the talmudic phrase "There is no constellation which determines a Jew's future"[6] to mean that a man may be born with various drives and personality traits, but by observing the Torah, he is able to lift himself above them and choose the proper path. He need not embrace *all* that he feels naturally drawn to. On the other hand, as we have seen from Rashi, he achieves his purpose and meaning in life by pursuing the *positive* aspects of his God-given personality. The Torah teaches him to choose and select what to embrace and what to reject.

The feminist critique is a multifaceted one. However, three

general attitudes seem to underlie much of it. The first is that significance is attached to those activities which are done in public and attract public recognition. Second, an act is significant to the degree that one is paid for it. Third, intellectual work is intrinsically superior to physical work.

Judaism categorically rejected all three attitudes. About the first, we have said much already in part 1. The Mishnah tells us:

> Akavyah ben Mehalel testified on four matters. The rabbis told him: "Change your mind on these matters and we shall appoint you as the head of the beth-din of Israel." He told them: "It is better that I be called a fool my entire life than I be called an evil man for one hour by God."[7]

The essential posture that lends value to a person's life is his posture before God, not his most exalted career plans, nor that which is viewed or commended by others. The *Shulḥan Arukh* begins: "'I have set the Lord always before me' [Ps. 16:8] is the essential principle of the Torah."[8] The constant realization that human actions take place before God, the source of all value, is the central motif that should color every moment in the life of a Jew. The approval and glory of public exposure should pale in comparison with God's approval.

The second point of view, which is also foreign to the Jewish mind, is that something is valuable to the degree that it commands a price. Activities should be intrinsically meaningful. That is why ideally one must not take money for the learning or teaching of Torah. An essential task must be pursued for its own sake, not for any remuneration that society may provide. The price tag is, at most, society's monetary evaluation of the activity, but this is far from expressive of its ultimate divine value. A price tag hardly measures essential value.

The achievement of financial independence has been a major aspect of the demand by women for the right to pursue careers. While the Halakhah provides the legal structure for women to have careers and to be financially independent, Jewish thought and society have consistently taken a negative view of such aspirations. The family is the basic unit of Jewish life, and it is meant to function in a unified manner. Man and wife unite through marriage and form "one flesh" (Gen. 2:24). Each partner in a marriage surrenders his independence for the sake of forming this unit; together, husband and wife form a functioning whole, separately, both are incomplete. One who does not wish to surrender his independence can never be truly married.

A number of detailed laws were enacted to protect a woman from being abused by her lack of financial independence and to guarantee her proper treatment. The Talmud expressed the underlying philosophy of these laws in its statement that a man must spend more money on his wife's needs than on his own.[9] In the event that the legal and moral strictures of the Jewish code failed, a woman was allowed to pursue financial independence, but this was always seen as a last resort, never as a goal.

So far as physical work is concerned, Judaism's attitude has always been one of the essential areas in which it has differed from many of its neighbor cultures. While Greece and Rome denigrated physical work and ascribed significance only to intellectual and leisurely pursuits, Judaism always saw in man's work the fulfillment of the divine directive to "fill the earth and conquer it" (Gen. 1:28). When Adam was expelled from Eden, the Torah tells us, "And God sent him out of the Garden of Eden to work the earth from whence he had been taken" (Gen. 3:23). Man conquers the world by his physical and intellectual efforts and thereby joins with God in the act of creation.

> Shmayah and Avtalyon received the tradition. . . . Shmayah said: "Love work." A man should love work and not despise it. Just as the Torah was given through a covenant, so was work given through a covenant. . . . R. Tarfon said that the Almighty

> did not cause His presence to dwell among Israel until they did work. R. Yehudah ben Beterah said that he who does not have work to do, if he has an empty field should go and cultivate it. . . . All this applies to important men and women and even to the unimportant.[10]

The Greeks glorified the intellectual and denigrated the physical, and hence could find no redeeming features in physical labor. As time passed, Rome increasingly became a slave economy and a leisure society, where physical labor was regarded as unbefitting the patrician class. However, the Jew viewed man as essentially a religious being enjoined to weld together the physical and the spiritual. The essential value of an act lay in its religious value, and this was independent of whether an act constituted intellectual or physical labor. Both intellectual and physical activities are valid means of self-expression, and neither is intrinsically superior to the other.[11]

While housework forms a significant part of a woman's work, this does not mean that a woman was meant to define herself primarily in terms of this aspect of her job. When the prophet Jonah was asked: "What is your work, and from which nation are you?" (Jonah 1:8), he answered: "I am a Hebrew and I fear the Lord, God of the heavens, who has made the sea and the dry land" (Jonah 1:9). Jonah's self-definition was exclusively in terms of his religious activities. His other deeds did not contribute to his self-definition. Most people spend most of their time performing the monotonous routine essential to their work. Authors spend countless hours on trivial research, editing manuscripts, correcting proofs, etc.; businessmen spend hours shuffling papers, preparing reports, etc. These nuisances are disregarded because of the essential value of the end product—the book published or the money earned—and the persons who perform such tasks define themselves in terms of the final result of their work, not the monotony of some of its routinized aspects.

The "occupation-housewife," as portrayed in the contemporary feminist literature, is truly an empty, sterile life.[12] If the end product to be achieved is merely waxed floors and whiter clothes, as Betty Friedan claims, then this is truly not a life for anyone but the most insipid of individuals. A Jewish woman, however, is expected to define herself in terms of her own praying, studying, doing of *ḥesed,* and creating of a Jewish home. Her other work is necessary for her essential tasks, but was never meant to serve as a means to her self-definition. Unfortunately, with the secularization of Jewish life in the United States and the concomitant secularization of the family, the role of the woman has been similarly secularized and reduced to a series of empty activities.

The secular life is an empty one for both men and women. Men try to fill the void in their lives by a frenetic pursuit of false goals, but none of these, when achieved, has the capacity to satisfy. Thus life remains essentially empty and meaningless. In his daily prayer, a Jew recites: "We pray that He will open up our hearts to His Torah and that He will place in our hearts His love and His fear so that we may perform His will and serve Him with a complete heart, so that we shall not strive for an empty existence, nor give birth to confusion." A life devoid of the fear and love of God is an empty, confused life. A man pursuing a career is given the opportunity to fool himself more easily than can a woman who remains at home.

The emptiness of "occupation-housewife," which has given the feminist credo such wide acceptance, draws upon yet another phenomenon of modern American life. Americans pursue independence and individualism with a mad passion.[13] The American's desire for his own home, his own car, etc., and his desire to be independent of his neighbors and friends, has undermined the security afforded by the extended family and a stable community. Every American, albeit he is totally dependent on the government, insists on being independent of those around him. He feels that he is part of nothing and experiences the anonymity so well described by Cox.[14] Men relieve this feeling of anonymity through their associations at work. On his job, each man is a member of a goal-oriented community. In her home, "occupation-housewife," as part of nothing, pursues nothingness, accompanied by no one. She has no community and lacks a specific and definite goal.

Jessie Bernard tells us that the mental health picture of "occupation-housewife" is a disaster.[15] This is hardly a surprise. Only the vacuous could fail to go mad continually pursuing nothingness, with no one to share that experience. The American genius for isolating women in small, boxlike dwellings, with no real goals and devoid of meaningful tasks, would frustrate and devastate the psyche of even the healthiest person.

But Eve's role as "mother of all mankind" need not be psychologically devastating and ultimately meaningless. Money and public acclaim need not be the only goals in life. The Jewish woman's primary goal should be her own religious well-being and the religious well-being of her family. But more essentially, *no* Jew is allowed to live by and for himself. *Every* Jew is required to live as part of a community. Judaism can only be fully experienced in a community. Cox noted that village life is fundamentally religious and city life secular. In a further sense, to be a religious Jew one must live not only for himself, not only for his family, but also for his community. To experience *ḥesed*, the root character trait demanded of every observant Jew, one must live as part of a larger unit. The pursuit of careers is not the only way to fight the anonymity of the city. Involvement in communal religious activity is certainly equally rewarding. If city living is essentially secular, we must not cooperate in this secularization of our lives. Rather, we must make greater efforts to establish strong, well-knit religious communities for ourselves.

However, the aspect of feminism that is probably most antithetical to Jewish values is the concept of career so prevalent in a large segment of feminist literature. A career is portrayed as an all-engrossing, self-justifying regimen to which all other pursuits must be subordinated.[16] We are led to believe that the only person who is truly human is the one who strives to satisfy the demands of his own success. Being oneself means, in this context, being answerable to no one but oneself and needing no one but oneself.

Such a pursuit of career not only portrays falsely the way most men lead their lives, but also denies the essence of the message of Judaism. A Jew's self-justification must always be defined in terms of his obligations to God and his fellow men. These obligations and relationships define his essence. One who lives by and for himself denies *ḥesed,* the very foundation of Judaism. Every Jew is answerable to God, to his people, and to those around him, and is judged by how he answers the demands they place upon him.

In the final analysis, one cannot simply say that careers for women are "permitted" or "forbidden." A woman's primary concern must be the religious well-being of her family. The religious life of a woman is a part of Jewish life and indispensable for Jewish survival. If a career is a primary dedication, the pursuit of a career is inconsistent with the ideals of Jewish womanhood. If, on the other hand, it is understood that a career is only a secondary consideration and remains subservient to the primary dedication of building a Jewish home, then a career is certainly not inconsistent with Jewish ideals. The considerations that enter into a specific career decision are similar to those that may determine a man's choice; i.e., the pursuit of *ḥesed* and to what degree specific worldly pursuits further the ultimate goal of *le'taken olam bemalkhut sh'*—to remake the world into a divine kingdom.

The contemporary and Jewish views of liberation are in one sense close and in another sense miles apart. On the one hand, both say that many forces act upon a person, and that he should be freed from undesirable tasks and obligations and enabled to get down to the essential tasks of life. The crux of the problem, though, is to define the objectionable forces that encroach upon a person's life and the essential tasks that he must get down to.

The Talmud tells us: "There is no truly free person except the one who involves himself in the study of Torah, for anyone who totally involves himself in the study of Torah is elevated."[17] A person is subject to a variety of forces—physical, psychological, and cultural. On the physical and psychological levels, everyone is subjected to forces which influence his decision-making in all spheres of his activity. By carefully regulating all activities, Judaism introduced order and discipline into every area of life. Before a knowledgeable Jew acts, he must always stop and ask himself: "May I or may I not?" "Should I or should I not?" Someone whose life is absolutely dominated by the Halakhah must always pause a moment before he acts in order to evaluate his actions. The "moment before" introduces order and discipline into his life. It enables him to exercise control of his actions and to overcome the tyranny of his physical and psychological drives. Once one can stop and consider every act, and if need be refrain from an act, although driven by every physical and psychological drive within him, he is on the road to liberation. He can control his actions and is not driven by forces outside his control. The Song of Songs says: "Your belly is a stack of wheat fenced with roses" (Song of Songs 7:3). The Midrash comments:

> R. Levi said, for example, a man, who did not marry until he was thirty or forty years, after the wedding when he comes to have relations with his bride and she tells him: "I saw a drop red as a rose," he separates immediately. Who has caused him not to come close to her? Which iron wall separates them? Which iron post is between them? Which snake has bitten him? Which scorpion has stung him so as not to come close to her? It is the words of the Torah, which are soft as the petals of the rose and it says: "And you shall not approach a woman in her menstrual

> period" [Lev. 18:19]. Similarly, consider the man to whom was brought a potful of delicacies and was told that some *ḥelev* [forbidden fat] has fallen in, and he withdraws his hand and does not taste of it. Who has caused him not to taste of it? Which snake has bitten him? Which scorpion has stung him not to come close and even taste it? The words of the Torah, which are as soft as the petals of the rose, which say: "Any *ḥelev* and any blood shall you not eat" [Lev. 3:17].[18]

The liberated man may enjoy relations with his bride and wife. He may enjoy all the pleasures of this world. But he must be freed from the tyranny of those drives which deprive him of essential freedom.

However, as powerful as are the physical and psychological forces which motivate a person, even more powerful are the cultural forces which act upon him. The implicit assumptions and values of the society around a person are invariably assimilated and accepted. The moment a value or concept, even an ephemeral cultural fad, is assimilated subconsciously into a person's cultural world view, it is very often accepted without question or critical analysis. Liberation also includes liberation from such tyranny. The vast majority of people accept these values without question as obvious and self-evident, without applying any critical analysis, and thus become subject to the tyranny of the few eloquent opinion-makers whose current fad is riding the wave of popular acceptance.

The Talmud says there is no liberated man except he who is totally involved in Torah. To be truly free, a person must first of all be freed from the tyranny of his physical, psychological, and cultural drives, and must get down to the essentials of life. For a Jew, the essentials of life lie in two directions: the realization and maximization of one's relationship with God, and the passing on of this message to others and to future generations. For the Jew, these are life's essential tasks. Other tasks, however important, lack their ultimacy.

To see the cultural fads of the day clearly, and to determine the degree to which they are consistent with these essential tasks and needs, it is necessary to be totally conversant with the Torah axiology. Deep and thorough knowledge is necessary. Anything short of this just will not do. That is why the Talmud uses the phrase *osek be'talmud Torah*—"preoccupied with the study of the Torah." Only this can suffice to focus the mind clearly on the essentials of life, to distinguish the essential from the irrelevant and permanent value from the transitory. To be in control of the various physical and psychological drives that act upon him, a Jew must be knowledgeable and must lead a life dominated by halakhic discipline. Both of these are required if the divine presence in life is to be felt.

The contemporary Jew is truly not liberated. How many Jews have a deep enough insight into their own tradition to free themselves from the tyranny of the cultural biases and crazes of current life and to dedicate themselves to essential tasks? How many can resist the pressures of public approval to be as truly free as Akavyah ben Mehalel? How many are free enough to judge their own worth by its essential value and not by society's dollars-and-cents price? The Jewish heroic act is played before God and for His approval. In the words of the Bible, "And God told Samuel: 'Do not look at his countenance, nor at his imposing height, for I have rejected him. For it is not what man sees [that is important]. For man looks with his eyes, but God looks at the heart'" (1 Sam. 16:7).

To the extent that feminism may become a vehicle for women to deepen their experience of Judaism, it is to be applauded. Many areas of genuine Jewish activity for women have fallen into neglect due to pressing historical and social exigencies. Prayer is incumbent upon women as it is upon men. Prayer expresses unqualified dependence upon God. Since women are as dependent upon God as men, it is imperative that women dedicate themselves to prayer. The Jewish woman was endowed with unique talents for inner experience and should develop that capacity in the direction of devotional activity.

Women are minimally obligated to pray twice daily, in the morning and in the afternoon. Evening prayers are optional for women. Devotional activities are an essential aspect of Jewish life. Unfortunately, the Greek glorification of intellect as the supreme value, and the denigration of the emotional life as inferior, if not despicable, has possessed the minds of many of today's intellectual elite. The subsequent denigration of devotional activity in general, and of prayer activity in particular has closed off this most fundamental area for both men and women. If prayer has declined in vibrancy for American Jewish men, who at least go through the formalities of prayer every day, it has declined still more for women, who have largely dropped prayer entirely. It is important that women take the prayer experience seriously and devote themselves to "the service of the heart."[19] The experience of prayer is an essential prerequisite for religious growth. One who has never confronted God in prayer has certainly not confronted Him in other areas of life.

The modern Jewish woman, educated with all the sophistication of twentieth-century culture, finds herself in the awkward position of being more conversant with alien cultures than with her own. To have a sophisticated view of everything else and a Sunday School knowledge of Judaism is an unforgivable crime. It is of the utmost importance that women deepen their knowledge of their Jewish heritage from a specifically Jewish perspective. In these two major areas, women should initially try to enhance their experience of Judaism.

However, if the women's rights movement seeks to eliminate the role differentiation so essential to Jewish life, our attitude must be that of Hillel of old.[20] Hillel was approached by a gentile who sought conversion to Judaism on the condition that he be appointed high priest. Hillel acceded to his request, but explained that the high priest must be a highly learned man. The gentile, lured by the glory of the high priesthood, agreed to dedicate himself to Torah study. Sometime later, when he had achieved a good knowledge of Judaism, the convert came to the verse "And the non-priest who comes close, [performs the Temple service] will be put to death" (Num. 1:51). He turned to Hillel and asked: "To whom does this refer?" Hillel replied: "It refers to any non-priest, even David, king of Israel, himself." The convert, now aware of the folly of his initial desire, agreed to dedicate himself to the service of God in the manner suitable to him. Divine service is a serious matter and must not be taken lightly. Role differentiation is an essential aspect of this service.

Priest, Levite, and Israelite; male and female—all of these together are dedicated to a single task, and that task can only be achieved if each performs his individual role.

Closing with the words of Maimonides: **וזהו דרך בני ישראל ובנות ישראל הקדושים והטהורים בזווגם ובדרכים אלו יהיה ישובן נאה ומשובח** "And this is the way of the sons and daughters of Israel, who are holy and pure in their relationship, and in these manners will their lives together be beautiful and praiseworthy."

Notes

Chapter 1

1. Gen. R. 1:1.

2. See Rashi to Exod. 20:2.

3. See, in a similar vein, R. Joseph B. Soloveichik, "Ish ha-Halakhah," *Talpioth*, vol. 1; idem, "Mah Dodekh Midod," *HaDoar* 42, no. 39 (1963). Also see the discussion in part II of this work regarding Maimonides' view of divine will and wisdom.

4. See Maimonides, *Hil. Teshuvah* 10:1–4 and *Commentary to the Mishnah, Sanh.*, chap. *Ḥelek* (in some editions this is chap. 10, in others chap. 11) throughout, but specifically at the beginning, in the discussion of the "fifth group of people." Although Maimonides speaks disparagingly of this motivation, he still includes it in the command to fear God. See *Sefer ha-Mitzvot*, positive commandment 4.

5. Ber. 4a.

6. Deut. R., ad loc.

7. See Ber. 13a; Maimonides, *Hil. Kriat Shema* 1:2.

8. Rudolf Otto, *The Idea of the Holy* (London, 1968), p. 5.

9. See Gen. R. 23:6 and *Matnot Kehunah*, ad loc. See also Gen. R. 14:3 in the same context.

10. Tosefta, Shev. 3:5.

11. Kid. 31a.

12. See Rashi on Gen. 1:1 and Gen. R. 1:4, among others. This idea occurs continually throughout the Midrash.

13. *Ber.* 7b.

Chapter 2

1. Gen. 1:27. See Maimonides, *Guide to the Perplexed* 1:1.

2. Gen. 2:7. See Naḥmanides, ad loc.

3. *Eruv.* 18a. This also seems to be the interpretation of the Septuagint; see *Meg.* 9a.

4. Raavad, Introduction of *Baal ha-Nefesh* Jerusalem: Mosad HaRav Kook, 1964).

5. This idea is not unique to the Raavad. It is commonly used by many scholars subsequent to him. The Vilna Gaon uses the image very often. The Raavad, though, seems to be the earliest source for the concept.

6. Gen. R. 18:2.

7. There are two aspects of *tzniut*—personal privacy and bodily privacy. We are concerned here only with personal privacy.

8. J.T. *Ber.* 5:1.

9. See *Shev.* 30a; Lev. R. 20:11; Num. R. 1:3; Mid. Tanḥ., *Bamidbar* 3, *Vayishlaḥ* 6.

10. Mid. *Tanḥ, Bamidbar* 3; Num. R. 1:3.

11. Num. R. 1:3.

Chapter 3

1. See J.T. *Yeb.* end of first chap., and *Avot* 2:8.
2. *Ket.* 62b; *Ned.* 50a.
3. Eccles. R. 7:7; see also B. T. *Shab.* 147b; *A R N* 14:6.
4. Gen. R. 17:7.

Chapter 4

1. Mid. Tanh., *Lekh Lekhob,* 9; Naḥmanides, *Commentary to the Pentateuch,* Gen. 12:6, 14:1, 26:1, 32:4, 15, 26, 33:18, 44:14, 48:2.
2. Rashi to Gen. 18:9.
3. Rashi to Gen. 21:12.
4. Exod. 1:15, 16.
5. Exod. R. 1:16.
6. Ibid. 1:17.
7. *Pirkei Rabbi Eliezer,* chap. 45.
8. Rashi to Num. 26:64.
9. Mid. Zutah to Ruth, ed. Buber, p. 54. In a more particular vein, see Pesa. 109b, *Sot.* 11b.

Chapter 5

1. This seems to be the meaning of Onkelos's translation.
2. Exod. 34:6.
3. *Hil. Megillah* 2:17.

4. Compare this with Ruth Benedict's concept of synergy. See, for instance, A. H. Maslow, *The Farther Reaches of Human Nature* (New York: Viking Press, 1971).

5. See *B. B.* 106.

6. This becomes very clear when one compares *Sheiltot* of R. Aḥai Gaon, nos. 62 and 147, both concerned with the command of charity.

7. See *Sifre* on Deut. 15:7.

8. Prov. 31:26.

9. *Suk.* 49b.

10. See *Yoma* 38a, *Suk.* 49b. For the לומד שלא לשמה, *lomed shelo li'shmoh,* see below, chap. 6., n. 5.

11. *Ket.* 62b, *Ned.* 50a.

Chapter 6

1. See the commentaries of both exegetes to Deut. 4:9.

2. This seems to be the interpretation of the talmudic statement (*Sot.* 21a): "Thus did R. Menaḥem ben Yossi teach about the verse 'For the mitzvah is like a candle, and the Torah is like light' [Prov. 6:21]. The Scriptures liken a mitzvah to a candle and the Torah to light to tell you that just as a candle gives light for a short while, so a mitzvah is protective for a short while. Just as light lasts forever, so too does Torah protect forever. Thus did the Scriptures say: 'As you walk shall it lead you.' This refers to this world. 'When you lie down, it shall guard over you.' This refers to death. 'When you wake it shall argue in your defence.' This refers to the hereafter. Another interpretation is that sin can cancel out the reward of a mitzvah but cannot cancel out the reward of Torah, as it says: 'Many waters cannot extinguish love' [Song of Songs 8:7] (and the chief demonstration of love is the learning of Torah). The Talmud then proceeds to say that the rewards for a man come from the learning of Torah, and for a woman from creating a Jewish family. See also *Ber.* 21a; Mid. Tanḥ., *Noah* 3.

3. According to many, the reward given to women is greater. See *Ber.* 17b and *Arukh Ha-Shulḥan* to *Yoreh Deah* 246.

4. The Bible describes man's three basic pleasure drives: "And when the woman saw that the tree was good for food and that it was a delight to the eye and that it was to be desired to make one wise" (Gen. 3:5). While a beast is driven only by a physical pleasure drive, a human being can be driven by physical pleasure, aesthetic pleasure, and intellectual pleasure. Judaism never ied man his pleasures. Quite the contrary! Anyone who eschews pleasure is viewed as a sinner who has found something objectionable in God's crea-

tion. The Talmud says: "The Nazirite who denies himself the pleasure of wine is called a sinner for this mildly ascetic posture, much more so those who deny themselves more essential pleasures" (*Ta'an.* 11a). The Yerushalmi says: "All men are destined to give account for all their eyes beheld of which they did not partake" (J.T. *Kid.* 4:12). But the drive to achieve pleasure must be tamed. The seeking of pleasure for pleasure's sake alone turns man into a self-seeking, self-involved being. One of the major thrusts of the halakhic way of life is to redeem the pleasure experience from its basically selfish nature. The experiencing of pleasure is not sinful; the selfish pursuit of it is. The selfish pursuit of pleasure, be it intellectual, aesthetic, or physical, will lead man to reject all moral restraints. "And you shall not go after your heart and after your eyes" (Num. 15:39) is interpreted by most authorities as limiting man from excessive pursuit of pleasure (see, for instance, *Sefer ha-Ḥinukh,* sec. 387). Naḥmanides sees this also in the command "And you shall be holy" (Lev. 19:2). This is one of the reasons that Judaism found it necessary to introduce religious motifs in all areas of the pleasure experience (see *Shaar ha-Kedushah* of the Raavad). There is no difference between these three areas. The aesthetic and intellectual experience per se do not produce moral excellence. One-third of our people was destroyed by a nation that excelled in the aesthetic and intellectual sphere. (For a more detailed analysis of this topic, see my forthcoming essay on Purim.)

5. See *Ber.* 17a; J.T. *Ber.* 1:2; Lev. R. 35:7. He who studies without the intent to practice would have been better off had he not been born.

6. Twelve months is the longest sentence given to the evil in the afterlife.

7. The relevance of the myrtle to the Sabbath has many interpretations. The most plausible is that the myrtle was used at weddings in ancient times. See *Sot.* 49b; Tosefta, *Sot.* 15:8; *Ket.* 17a. The Sabbath symbolized to the Jew both the wedding of God to the Jewish people and, more commonly, the wedding of the Jewish people to the Sabbath day. The song Lekhoh Dodi, recited on Friday nights, is based on this image. To R. Shimon, the myrtle represented the absolute devotion of the Jewish people to their divine calling when involved in worldly pursuits.

8. The command to observe the Sabbath is one of the Ten Commandments, but its wording differs significantly in the two versions of the Ten Commandments. In Exod. 20:8, the term *Zakhor* ("Remember") is used; in Deut. 5:12, *Shamor* ("Keep") is used. These two facets of the Sabbath command were commemorated by the two myrtles.

9. *Shab.* 33b.

10. The answer to this question we find, of course, in R. Shimon's comment to his son upon leaving the cave the first time: "My son, it is enough for the world to have two people such as you and me totally involved in the

Torah." For the continuation of the Jewish tradition, it is not necessary to have the entire populace totally involved in the constant learning of Torah.

11. *Ber.* 35b.

12. See in this context *San.* 99a and Maimonides, *Hil. Talmud Torah* 3:13.

13. This does not mean that the man who does not dedicate his life to the study of Torah is exempt from the study of Torah. Maimonides says: "Every Jewish man, whether poor or rich, healthy or sick, young or old . . . is required to set aside time every day and night for the study of Torah (*Talmud Torah* 1:8). While one is not necessarily required to dedicate himself completely, he is required to set aside some definite time every day for the study of Torah.

14. Maimonides, *Shmittah ve'Yovel* 13:13.

15. Gen. R. 99:11. A similar midrash is found in Lev. R. 25:1–2.

16. *Yoreh Deah* 246.

17. *Ber.* 17b. See p. 17 for another interpretation of this passage.

18. *B. B.* 9a.

19. There are variants in the manuscript of the Tosefta as regards this point. The text in the standard printed version and the text of the Vilna Gaon of Tosefta *Yev.* 8:2 read: "And a woman is permitted to remain unmarried." Zuckermandel reads as above, according to the Erfurt manuscript. Some manuscripts read, though, that a woman is not allowed to remain unmarried; see, for instance, the Riaz, as quoted by the *Shiltei Gibborim* at the beginning of the sixth chapter of *Yevamot.*

In reality, though, all agree as to the interpretation of the law. Maimonides, in *Isurei Biah* 21:26, says: "A woman should not remain without a husband so that she not become suspect of immoral behavior." A man is required to marry as a result of two distinct positive commandments. First, a man is required to enter the married state per se (see Maimonides, positive commandment 213), and second, a man is required to procreate. A woman is excused from both of these commandments for a variety of reasons. Besides those mentioned in the text, Rabbi Meir Simḥah (d. 1926) (*Meshekh Ḥokhmah* to Gen. 9:1) said that a woman could not be required to procreate since childbirth presents a danger to her life. The Torah left it up to the woman whether or not to accept this danger upon herself. However, Maimonides says, in view of the fact that the Torah recognized the reality of the sexual drives of both man and woman, it said that, from a purely practical point of view, it is not right for a woman to remain alone. The Vilna Gaon interprets the Tosefta as referring to the positive commandments to marry and procreate, while the Riaz interprets the Tosefta as referring to the more practical statement.

20. See Prov. 31:10–31.

21. *Meg.* 14b.

22. Mid. Zutah to Ruth, ed. Buber, p. 54, says: "Each generation is redeemed for the righteous women of that generation." In a more particular vein, see *Pes.* 109b, *Sot.* 11b.

Chapter 7

1. The Talmud in *Kid.* 29b bases this on the verse "And you shall teach it to your sons" (Deut. 11:19). Women are not bound to study or to teach, nor are men bound to teach them.

2. *Sot.* 20a.

3. This seems to be the interpretation of Maimonides' term דברי הבאי *dibrey habai*. See also the comments of the Meiri, ad loc.

4. Maimonides, *Hil. Yesodei ha-Torah* 4:13.

5. Maimonides, *Hil. Talmud Torah* 1:13.

6. The word מכוונות *mekhuvanot* seems to indicate readiness rather than capability. To translate as "capability" would contradict the above quotation from *Yesodei ha-Torah*.

7. This seems to be the interpretation adopted by the Rama to *Yoreh Deah* 246:6.

8. *Sot.* 21b–22a.

9. R. Avraham Danzig, introduction to *Ḥaye Adam*.

10. *Avot* 2:6.

11. See *Sanh.* 71a, 99a–b; see esp. *Likutei Amorim Tanya* of R. Shneur Zalman of Ladi, esp. chaps. 1, 4, 5; Maimonides, *Hil. Teshuvah* 10:6; *Yesodei ha-Torah* 4:13.

12. See *S. A. Yoreh Deah* 246:6 in Rama.

13. *Sot.* 21b D"H *Ben Azai*. See introduction of *Eglai Tal*, where an alternative interpretation of this law is adopted. *Beth Halevi*, vol. 1, sec. 6, concurs with *Eglai Tal*. Also see *Avnei Nezer* to *Yoreh Deah* 2:352.

14. *B. K.* 38a.

15. *Beur ha-Grah* to *Yoreh Deah* 246:6 quotes *B. K.* 38a as evidence of the fact that the study of Torah by women is a meritorious act.

16. Maimonides, *Hil. Talmud Torah* 1:13.

17. R. Ḥayim Yosef Dovid Azulay (Ḥidah), *Tuv Ayin*, (Husiatyn, 1904), sec. 4.

18. *Eruv.* 53, *Pes.* 62.

19. *San.* 94b.

20. *Perishah* to *Tur, Yoreh Deah* 246:6.

21. Responsa of R. Yehudah Aszod (Lemberg, 1873), sec. on *Yoreh Deah* 48.

22. R. Shmuel ben R. Elḥanan Yaakov Rakvalti, *Maayan Ganim* (Venice, 1553). This responsum is quoted in *Torah Temimah* to Deut. 11:19 and in R. Gedaliah Felder, *Yesodei Yeshurun* (Toronto, 1954), 1:137.

23. *Mesharet Moshe* to *Talmud Torah* 1:13, p. 15b; *Torah Temimah* to Deut. 11:19; *Yafeh LaLev*, vol. 3, in comments to *Yoreh Deah* 246. These authorities make no attempt to resolve the paradox.

24. R. Israel Meir ha-Cohen, *Likutei Halakhot, Sotah* 20a, p. 11a.

25. R. Zalman Sorotzkin, *Moznaim la-Mishpat* (Jerusalem, 1968), sec. 42.

26. Besides the above-mentioned authorities, lists of others who concur can be found in Felder, *Yesodei Yeshurun*, and R. Eliezer Waldenberg, *Tzitz Eliezer*, vol. 9, sec. 3. In specific, see R. Abraham Neumark, *Eshel Avraham* (Tel-Aviv, 1954), 2:269–70.

27. *Nid.* 45b.

28. Ritva, ad loc.

29. *Kid.* 80b, *Shab.* 33b; see Tos. to *Hul.* 2a, who uses it also in reference to squeamishness at the sight of blood. Naḥmanides, in *Torat ha-Adam*, uses it in reference to an over-emotional response in the face of death. The last two references, although within the same context, are minority opinions and are rejected as bases for halakhic decisions.

30. See above, p.18.

Chapter 8

1. *B.K.* 15a.

2. Maimonides, *Hil. Avodat Kokhavim* 12:13.

3. Abudrahm, sec. on Weekday Prayers. See, in addition, *Magen Avot* by R. Shimon Duran 2:6 and in *Shitat ha-Kadmonim* to Baba Kama ed. M.Y. Blau, New York 1976 p. 334.

4. See Meiri to *Ber.* 11a.

5. *Torah Temimah* to Exod. 13:9.

6. *B.K.* 15a. This point is made in dramatic fashion by *Seder Eliyahu Rabbah* chap. 9. The question is raised why did Deborah prophesy and save Israel when Phineas, the High Priest was still alive. The answer is given. "I call heaven and earth to testify that whether Jew or gentile, man or woman, whether male-slave or female slave, the Divine Presence rests on each one according to his actions."

7. Maharal, *Drush al ha-Torah,* included in *Sifrei Maharal* (Jerusalem, 1971) in the volume with *Be'er ha-Golah,* p. 27a.

8. *Ber.* 17a.

9. See above, p. 32 for a different interpretation of this talmudic passage.

10. R. Samson Raphael Hirsch, *Commentary to Leviticus* (New York, 1971), 23:43.

11. *Yalkut Shimoni* to 1 Sam. 1:13.

Chapter 9

1. Rashi to *Eruv.* 96 and *R. H.* 33a.

2. Commentary to *S. A. Oraḥ Ḥayim* 489:1.

3. *Ber.* 28a.

4. This equation is disputed by *Minḥat Ḥinukh,* sec. 306.

5. *Ḥaye Adam,* Laws of Rosh HaShanah 141:7, explicitly extends this to shofar.

6. See *Eruv.* 96a, *R. H.* 33a.

7. *Hil. Tzitzit* 3:9.

8. Rama to *Oraḥ Ḥayim* 589:6.

9. See *R.H.* 28a; Rashi D"H *Lo Lehonot Nitnu.*

10. The phrase "all of the" appears in the text of the Meiri (see Meiri to *Ber.* 60b) and in the text of the Ravyah (see Ravyah to *Ber.* 146, p. 140). However, even if the text is simply "not commanded in mitzvot," the phrase "all of the" is implicitly assumed.

11. Tosefta, *Ber.* 6:23.

12. *The Hirsch Siddur* (Jerusalem and New York: Feldheim, 1972).

13. I have never seen this idea in print, but have heard it from a variety of people.

14. *Eruv.* 13b.

15. Compare with *Ber.* 10b.

16. The fact that this rule is derived from the *gezerah shavah* of *lah lah me-ishah* proves nothing. A *gezerah shavah* does not necessarily presuppose any relationship between the two concepts other than similarity in word. This

is more than obvious to anyone who has ever handled talmudic discussions that revolve around *gezerah shavah*. It is implicit in the Talmud in *B.K.* 15a.

17. See Maimonides, *Issurei Biah* 14:9. A slave had the option of deciding whether or not he wanted to accept this partial conversion. He could not remain as a slave if he did not willfully accept this status. See also *Avadim* 8:12.

18. *Issurei Biah* 12:11.

19. Ibid. 13:12; *Yeb.* 47b.

20. See Tos. to *Yeb.* 47b D''H *Sham.*

21. See, for instance, *B.K.* 88a, *San.* 86a, where the phrase *aḥikha hu be-mitzvot* is used.

22. That a non-Jew is excluded is in reality stated in a verse in Deut. 17:15. The Talmud utilizes this fact continually. See, for instance, the above quotation and also, for example, *B.M.* 111b, *Bek.* 13b. See also Maimonides, *Genevah* 9:6, *Edut* 9:4. Whether or not partial obligation is sufficient is a problem in *B.K.* 88a, *San.* 86a, *J.T. San.* 11:2. The law is generally accepted that *aḥiv* means full obligation. See Maimonides *Edut* 9:4 and *Genevah* 9:6. While a cursory glance at *B. K.* 88a would indicate that partial obligation is sufficient for *aḥiv*, and that a slave's disqualification from testimony is from a source other than partial obligation, Maimonides, *Edut* 9:4, is explicit that for both sides of the dispute, the sole criterion is degree of obligation.

23. See Maimonides, *Edut* 9:2, *Genevah* 9:6.

24. This does not preclude self-defense, which is explicitly mentioned in Exod. 22:1. A person who attempts to murder eo ipso forfeits his own life.

25. *Sanh.* 74a. See, in this context, the quotation from *Seder Eliyahu Rabbah* on chap. 8; f.n. 6.

26. Rachel Adler, "The Jew Who Wasn't There: *Halakhah* and the Jewish Woman," *Davka,* Summer 1971.

27. *Ber.* 27b; Maimonides, *Hil. Tefillah* 1:6.

28. *Sefer ha-Ḥinukh* 31, 32, 85.

29. Ibid., 313, 315, 316, 317.

30. Ibid., 9, 10, 11, 19, 20, 21, 297, 298, 300, 301, 485.

31. Ibid., 308, 309.

32. Maimonides, *Hil. Ḥannukah* 3:4.

33. Maimonides, *Hil. Purim* 1:1.

34. *Sefer ha-Ḥinukh* 384.

35. See *Oraḥ Ḥayim* 417:1 and in various commentaries ad loc.

36. *Sefer ha-Ḥinukh* 321,322.

37. Maimonides, *Hil. Shofar* 2:1.

38. Maimonides, *Hil. Sukah* 6:1.

39. Maimonides, *Hil. Lulav* 7:19.

40. Maimonides, *Hil. Tzitzit* 3:9.
41. Maimonides, *Hil. Tefillin* 4:13.
42. Maimonides, *Hil. Kriat Shema.*
43. *Oraḥ Ḥayim* 38:3.
44. *Mekhiltah* to Exod. 20:1.
45. *Sefer ha-Ḥinukh* 418, 432.
46. Maimonides, *Hil. Kriat Shema* 4:1.
47. *Sefer ha-Ḥinukh* 25, 296, 417, 418, 432, 433.
48. *Shab.* 88b.
49. See Naḥmanides, *Commentary to the Torah,* Deut. 1:18.

Chapter 10

1. Lev. Rab. 20:7.
2. This sense of superiority resulted in an arrogant attitude toward Moses and Aaron. Furthermore, they refused to marry. They were apparently incapable of finding mates whom they could consider peers.
3. See in this context the commentary of R. Naftali Tzvi Yehudah Berlin (Netziv) to Song of Songs 1:2; also, the commentaries of Naḥmanides and Ibn Ezra to Deut. 12:30.
4. Rashi to above, Raavad to *Mamrim* 2:4.
5. *Hil. Mamrim* 2:8 The fact that Maimonides limits his comments to a legally constituted beth-din was pointed out to me by my teacher, Rabbi Joseph B. Soloveichik.
6. *Avot* 1:2.
7. *Commentary to the Torah,* Deut. 4:2. See also *Aderet Eliyahu* to Deut. 13:1.
8. *Kid.* 31a.
9. *J.T., Shab.* 1:2 (7a).
10. Ritva to *Kid.* 31a. See also *Ḥidushei ha-Ramban, ad loc.*.
11. See comments of the *Korban ha-Edah* to the Yerushalmi.
12. See *Tradition* 14, no. 2 (Fall 1973), p. 126.
13. Lev. R. 27:10.
14. *San.* 32b.
15. *B. K.* 88a.

Chapter 11

1. Sören Kierkegaard, *The Sickness Unto Death* (Anchor Books), p. 159.

2. R. Samson Raphael Hirsch, *Commentary to Psalms* 119:19 and also Rashi to Gen. 1:27.

Chapter 12

1. See S. Angus, *Religious Quest of the Graeco-Roman World* (New York, 1929), p. 62. In a similar vein, see *Interpreter's Bible,* 7:85; S. Angus, *Environment of Early Christianity,* (New York, 1915), pp. 181–85.

2. 1 Cor. 7.

3. This appears even among Greco-Jewish thinkers like Philo. For example, see Philo, *Migration of Abraham* 16:89 (in Loeb Classical Library ed. of Philo, trans. F.H. Colson and G. H. Whitaker [Cambridge: Harvard University Press, 1932], 3:183). While the dualism of Greek thought is clearly evident in Philo, the Jewish emphasis on fulfillment of the specific commandments is also present.

4. For a detailed, thorough analysis of this topic, see R. Joseph B. Soloveichik, "Ish ha-Halakhah", *Talpiot* 1, pp. 671–76. The Mishnah in *Avot* 4:22 summarizes this attitude in its statement: "One hour involved in Torah and mitzvot in this world is more exalted and beautiful than the entire life in the hereafter."

5. After death there is no progress, no achievement of higher levels, as the Talmud says: "He who has prepared himself before the Sabbath, eats thereof on the Sabbath" (*A.Z.* 3a). This does not denigrate life after death. The afterlife is the ultimate reward, but it is also a spiritually static existence with no opportunity for further religious growth.

6. A full discussion of the necessity for, and role of, law in Judaism will appear in my forthcoming essay, "The Tragedy of Saul." However, after all is said and done, Judaism is legalistic because, in point of fact, the divine will did reveal itself in terms of law. See also *Shiurei HaRav: A Conspectus of the Public Lectures of Rabbi Joseph B. Soloveichik* (New York, 1974), pp. 38–46.

7. *B. M.* 115a.

8. See Tos. to *Sotah* 14a D"H Kedai who interprets the Talmud in *B. M.* in this manner.

9. Deut. 22:6–7.

10. *Ber.* 33b.

11. *Ber.* 33b.

12. Naḥmanides to Deut. 22:6–7.

13. *Moreh Nevukhim* 3:48.

14. Ibid. 3:13 and 3:26.

15. Ibid. 3:27

16. This is a paraphrase of Exod. 19:21–22.

17. Maimonides, *Meilah* 8:8.

18. See Gersion Appel, *A Philosophy of Mitzvot* (New York: Ktav, 1975), pp. 22–24.

19. R. Samson Raphael Hirsch, *Commentary to Psalms,* (New York: Feldheim, 1966), introduction to chap. 119.

20. See Moshe Meiselman, "Women and Judaism: A Rejoinder" *Tradition* 3 (Fall 1975).

Chapter 13

1. See Rachel Adler, "The Jew Who Wasn't There," *Davka,* Summer 1971. On page 7 she says: "That women, children and slaves have limited credibility in Jewish law is demonstrated by the fact that their testimony is inadmissible in a Jewish court." On page 8 she claims: "Women are classed as inadmissible witnesses in the same category with gamblers, pigeon racers and other characters of unsavory repute." The same line of reasoning is followed in Paula Hyman, 'The Other Half: Woman in Jewish Tradition," *Conservative Judaism,* Summer 1972.

2. *Shev.* 34a.

3. Maimonides, *Edut* 4:1.

4. *Kesef Mishnah* to *Rotzeaḥ U'Shmirat Nefesh* 6:5.

5. Maimonides, *Edut* 5:3.

6. What prima facie seems to be an unworkable system of justice was complemented by other factors which allowed for punishment to provide for the smooth running of society. See Maimonides, *Rotzeaḥ U-Shmirat Nefesh* 4:8, 9; *Melakhim* 3:10; *Sanhedrin* 24:4.

7. *B. B.* 159a.

8. Maimonides, *Edut* 13:15.

9. Maimonides, *Melakhim* 3:7. See Rabbenu Ḥananel to *Yomah* 74b for an unusual interpretation of this disqualification.

10. See *Kesef Mishnah* to *Melakhim* 3:7.

11. The phrase is *lo meyid,* "cannot testify." A high priest must testify in a case involving the king (see *Klei ha-Mikdash* 5:8)

12. Maimonides, *Edut* 9:1, 2.

13. *Zev.* 103 a D"H *Ain.*

14. *Shaalot u-Teshuvot ha-Rashba ha-Meyuḥasot le'ha-Ramban,* no. 74.

15. Maimonides, *Sanhedrin* 18:6.

16. *San.* 9b D"H *Liritzonoh.*

17. See above, p. 73, fn.

18. *B. K.* 88a; Maimonides, *Edut* 9:4.

19. See above, also *Hagahot Asheri* to *Git.* 1:10.

20. *Edut* 9:2.

21. *Zev.* 103a D"H *Ain.*

22. In all the places in the Talmud that *aḥiv* excludes slaves and non-Jews, it is never applied to women. The Talmud deduces the exclusion of women from witness from another source; see *Kesef Mishnah* to *Edut* 9:2.

23. *Ket.* 72a.

24. *Ker.* 11b; Maimonides, *Shegogot* 3:2, *Sanhedrin* 16:6.

25. See *Shev.*, chaps. 6 and 7; Maimonides, *To'ain Venit'an* 1:1, 2.

26. Maimonides, *To'ain Venit'an* 2:1.

27. Ibid., 2:2.

28. Maimonides, *Sanhedrin* 24:1.

29. *Ḥosehn Mishpat* 35:14.

29a. Two midrashic sources discuss woman's disqualification as a witnes. *Pirkei Rabbi Eliezer* (chap 14) includes this as one of the nine consequences of the mutual sin of Adam and Eve. It is not clear, at all, what this disqualification shares in common with such things as menstruation, childbirth, etc. Furthermore, a similar list in the Talmud (Eruvin 100b) does not include the issue of testimony. The medieval midrash *Yalkut Shimoni* quotes an earlier midrash concerning the story of the prophecy to Abraham that Sarah would bear him a son. In response to this prophecy, Sarah laughed. When questioned by Abraham, Sarah denied laughing (Gen. 18:9–16). The midrash comments, "From here we see that women are disqualified to testify." The reasoning behind the midrashic comment is obscure. If one would intepret it to mean that women have no credibility, this comment would be in opposition not only to the wealth of material quoted in the text, but also to the entire structure of Jewish laws of credibility and testimony. In fact, there is no clear explanation of these two statements in the midrashic sources. Most important, however, these statements have been accorded total silence by all subsequent authorities. This certainly indicates that they do not lie in the mainstream of Jewish thought, whatever their proper interpretation may be.

30. See Maimonides, positive commandment 178.

31. See Maimonides, negative commandment 297.

32. See *Shev.* 30 and the Tosafot there *D"H Kol.* See also Git. 41, *Ket.* 74b.

Chapter 14

1.*Kid.* 35a.

2. See above, fn. to p. 73.

3. See, for instance, Maimonides, *Ishut* 12:1, 2.

4. See, for instance, ibid., 12:4.

5. *Ket.* 63a.

6. *Hasagot ha-Ravad al ha-Rif* to *Ket.* 63a (26a in Vilna edition); Rashba, ad loc.

7. Tos., *D"H Rav,* ad loc.

8. *Beit Shmuel* to *Even ha-Ezer* 80:21; *Piskei Din shel Batei Din ha-Rabanim be-Yisrael* [Decisions of Israeli rabbinic courts], ed. Katz and Glasner, vol. 2, p. 2 (decision of 22 Tevet 5717).

9. *Responsa of R. Meir of Rothenburg,* ed. Rabinowitz (Lemberg, 1860), sec. 57; *Hagahot Maimonyot, Ḥovel U'Mazik* 4:3.

Chapter 15

1. The laws governing this situation are found in *Ket.* 86b–87a. Many responsa deal with such arrangements. See, for instance, *Shaalot u-Teshuvot ha-Rashba ha-Meyuḥasot le'ha-Ramban,* no. 5; responsum of Raavad in *Responsae of the Sages of Provence* (ed. Schreiber), no. 36. Since there were generally competing claims between the heirs and the widow, the prevailing practice was to appoint a third party. However, it was not uncommon for a widow to be put in charge when such competing claims did not create a problem.

2. My source for much of the legal material is Thomas E. Atkinson, *Wills* (2nd ed., 1953). On the historical basis of wills, see Atkinson, pp. 30–36.

3. See Connor, "The Nature of Succession," 8 *Fordham Law Review,* p. 152.

4. Bigelow, "Theory of Post-Mortem Disposition: Rise of the English Will," 11 *Harvard Law Review,* p. 70. For a discussion of this point of view, see Atkinson, *Wills.* For a reaction against this view, see Connor, "Nature of Succession."

5. Atkinson, *Wills,* pp. 104–5, 107.

6. Ibid., p. 109.

7. There is some doubt as to the efficacy of any act of a *goses,* someone on the brink of death. If the disposition can be accomplished without his act, e.g., by a previously appointed agent, there is no doubt as to his ability to dispose of property. See Rosh, *Kid.* 4:16.

8. Due to the complex system of inheritance where there are no descendants, the only person who can have no heirs is a convert who leaves no descendants. His property becomes *hefker,* ownerless, upon his death.

9. See *B.B.* 175a.

10. See ibid. 149a and also 147a.

11. See *B.M.* 19b and Tos. D"H *Vehoh.* See Maimonides, *Zekhiah u-Matanah* 12:14. The *Kesef Mishnah,* ad loc., points out that there is no real difference between Maimonides and Rabbenu Tam other than the technical wording of the contract.

12. See *Ḥoshen Mishpat* 281:7.

13. See Deut. 21:17.

14. See Num. 27:8.

15. See Maimonides, *Ishut* 10:7.

16. See *Kid.* 13b.

17. See *B.B.* 126b in the Ran and the Rashba. The comments of the Rashbam are rejected by virtually everyone.

18. See *B.M.* 16a.

19. See *B.B.* 175b, 176a.

20. See Maimonides, *Malveh ve-Loveh* 18:1, and in *Magid Mishnah,* ad loc.

21. See Maimonides, *Ishut* 17:1–8.

22. See *B.B.* 139b.

23. Maimonides, *Ishut,* chaps. 10–25.

24. *Even ha-Ezer* 113.

25. See *B.B.* 139b.

26. See Rabbenu Gershom, *B.B.* 141a.

27. Every legal system is necessarily solicitous of creditors since this encourages the granting of credit. The Halakhah abounds in laws whose purpose is שלא תנעול דלת בפני לוים *sheloh tinol delet bifnei lovim*—"so as not to close the door in front of debtors." However, whereas daughters and widows have the status of creditors, most laws for the benefit of creditors also apply to them; this means that they cannot be pushed aside by other creditors.

28. *Git.* 48b.

29. *B.B.* 141a.

30. The concept of an heir per se does not exist in the Anglo-American system. All property is disposed of by will. If the decedent did not write a will and dies intestate, it is considered as if the state wrote the will for him. But ultimately it is a will. The state is concerned only with the orderly transfer of property and hence does not discuss inheritance of self.

31. *B.B.* 141a.

32. See Maimonides, *Melakhim* 1:7.

33. See *Sotah* 11a; *B.B.* 116a, 141a.

34. Num. 36; see *Ta'an.* 30b.

35. See Maimonides, *Shmittah ve'Yovel* 13:12.

Chapter 16

1.This is the essence of the *gezerah shavah* לה לה מאשה *lah lah me'ishah*. See *Kid.* 2a.

2. See *Ḥidushei ha-Ramban* to *Kid.* 16a.

3. *Ma'aser Sheni* 1:5, 3:12. There is no transfer of ownership in *Ma'aser Sheni*, even according to the opinion that מעשר שני ממון גבוה *ma'aser sheni mamon govohah;* see Maimonides, *Ma'aser Sheni* 3:24, 25, for a clear proof of this.

4. *Avot* 6:11–13.

5. See *Kid.* 5a. This point that the contract of marriage differs from others was really first made by Tos. *D"H Uminayin*, ad loc.

6. See Meiri to *Git.* 9a, Rashba to *Kid.* 6b *D"H Ey Naymah.* A list of authorities is given by Rabbi K. Kahane, *Theory of Marriage in Jewish Law* (Leiden: Brill, 1966), pp. 28 ff.

7. For a full discussion and comparison of English and Jewish law, see Kahane, *Theory of Marriage in Jewish Law.*

8. Maimonides, *Ishut* 3:11.

9. Rama to *Even ha-Ezer* 154:3, *Sefer Agudah* recommends chopping off the hands of wife-beaters.

10. *Kid.* 2a.

11. This is derived from the biblical phrase ספר המקנה *sefer ha-makneh*, Jer. 32:11, 12.

12. This is deduced from Deut. 22:13.

13. *Kid.* 2b.

14. The entire corpus of rabbinic literature is devoid of the idea that the man is the initiator of the marriage contract because of some second-class status of women.

15. See in this regard *Yeb.* 62b.

16. See Tos. to *Sotah* 14a D"H *Kedai.*

17. See Raavad, quoted by Rashba to *Kid.* 2b.

18. A puzzling fact that I have never seen explained is the difference in Jewish law between divorce between Jewish partners and divorce between non-Jewish partners. Adultery is a capital crime for non-Jews living under the jurisdiction of Jewish law. Hence, the law was required to define divorce for non-Jews. The Midrash (Gen. R. 18:8) presents three views: divorce is impossible, divorce is dependent exclusively on the wife, divorce is by either party. Maimonides decides: "And from what time on will the wife of his friend be considered as a divorcée? From the time he sends her from his house or when she leaves his house and goes out on her own. For non-Jews do not have a document of divorce and it does not depend upon him alone, but

anytime he or she wants to leave the other, they are divorced" (Maimonides, *Hil. Melakhim* 9:8). It is a puzzling fact indeed that Jewish divorce differs in this way from non-Jewish divorce. But it does show that the structure of Jewish divorce cannot be blithely explained away by reference to an implicit theory of male dominance.

19. See *Ket.* 11a, 39b, 54a; *Yeb.* 89a.

20. See *Yeb.* 63b; *J.T., Ket.* 11:3.

21. The Talmud presents the reaction of a truly religious person to such occurrences. Just as when a man finds himself oppressed by illness or other deviant behavior of the physical world, he realizes that he must see in it the divine will and accept it as that, so too someone who sees the divine will expressed not only in the physical laws, but in the moral ones as well, will of necessity accept such adversity as divine will. Just as the acceptance of disease as part of the divine scheme does not preclude fighting disease, so too the acceptance of such perversity as part of the divine scheme does not preclude fighting it. See *B.M.* 38b.

22. Maimonides, *Hil. Gerushin* 2:20.

23. Ibid.

24. See in this context R. Elyakim Elinson, "Siruv Latet Get," *Sinai* 69, nos. 3–4 (1971): 135 ff.

Chapter 17

1. The source material for the rabbinic rejection of annulment and conditional marriage is contained in R. Yehudah Lubetsky, *Ain Tnai be'Nisuin* (Vilna, 1930). In addition, the entire matter is discussed thoroughly in Abraham Chaim Freiman, *Seder Kiddushin ve'Nisuin* (Jerusalem: Mosad Harav Kook, 1945); R. Elyakim Elinson, "Siruv Latet Get," *Sinai* 69, nos. 3–4 (1971): 135 ff.; R. Nisan Zaks "Kiddushin Al Tnai," *Noam* 1 (1958): 52 ff.

2. See Maimonides, introduction to *Yad Ḥazakah*. See in this connection *Shaalot u-Teshuvot ha-Rosh* 43:8.

3. Maimonides, *Hil. Gerushin* 9:25.

4. R. Menachem M. Kasher, "Be'Inyan Tnai bi'Nisuin," *Noam* 11 (1968): 346.

5. *Yeb.* 90b, 110a; *Git.* 33a, 73a; *B. B.* 48b; *Ket.* 3a.

6. "Recent Additions to the *Ketubah*," *Tradition* 2, no. 1 (Fall 1959): 93–119.

7. "Self-Imposed Constraint in Divorce," *Noam* 1 (1958): 287–312.

8. *Rama* to *Even ha-Ezer* 134:4.

9. A. Leo Levin and Meyer Kramer, *New Provisions in the Ketubah* (New York: Yeshiva University, 1955). Another article,"Civil Enforceability of Religious Antenupital Agreements," which appeared in 23 *University of Chicago Law Review*, p. 122, also demonstrates the legal tenuousness of the Rabbinical Assembly agreement.

10. Levin and Kramer, op. cit., p. 3.

11. *Proceedings of the Rabbinical Assembly* 32 (1968): 229–41.

12. 138 N.Y.S. 2d 366.

13. 344 N.Y.S. 2d 482.

14. Ibid.

15. 356 N.Y.S. 2d 672.

16. 348 N.Y.S. 2d 61.

17. 36 D.L.R. (3d) 447.

18. 42 D.L.R. 3d 550.

Chapter 18

1. I have seen this article only in quotation by Roland B. Gittelsohn, "Women's Lib and Judaism," *Midstream* 17 (October 1971): 51–58.

2. See, for instance, Rachel Adler, "The Jew Who Wasn't There," *Davka*, Summer 1971, pp. 8–9.

3. Included in Raavad, *Baal ha-Nefesh* (ed. Mosad Harav Kook, 1964), p. 162.

4. See Rabbi C. Chavel, in *Kitvei ha-Ramban*, pp. 315–19, and G. Scholem, in *Kiryat Sefer* 21, pp. 179-86, for proper ascription of authorship.

5. This refers to Maimonides.

6. *Kitvei ha-Ramban*, ed. Rabbi C. Chavel (Jerusalem: Mosad Ha Rav Kook, 1964), 2:323.

7. See Pinchas Stolper, *Tzniut: The Road to Responsible Jewish Adulthood*, for an excellent treatment of this topic.

8. *Git.* 90a; Maimonides, *Gerushin* 10:21.

9. *Ned.* 20b.

10. Raavad, *Baal ha-Nefesh*, p. 121.

11. R. Menaḥem Recanti, *Taamei ha-Mitzvot*, sec. on procreation.

12. Raavad, *Baal ha-Nefesh*, p. 116.

13. Maimonides, *Hilk. Ishut* 14:1–2.

14. See *Pes.* 72b, esp. in Rashi; *Eruv.* 100b; Raavad, *Baal ha-Nefesh*, p. 124; *Sefer Mitzvot Katan*, no. 285; *Sh. A. Oraḥ Ḥayim* 240:1. Also see R. Ḥaim Yosef David Azulay, *Pnei David, Mishpatim*, sec. 8, and *Marit ha-Ayin* by the same author to *Nid.* 31; R. Yishayahu Asher Zelig Margolyot, *Daat ha-Kedoshah*, p. 138.

15. Ibid.

16. *Pes.* 72b.

17. See *Ber.* 62a, *Eruv.* 100b, *Hag.* 5b; Raavad, *Baal ha-Nefesh,* p. 119; Maimonides, *Hil. Deot.* 5:4; *S. A., Oraḥ Ḥayim* 240:1.

18. This is eliminated in some texts in conformity with *S. A.Even ha-Ezer* 25:1. See Margolyot, op. cit., p. 72.

19. See *Yomah* 1:1 (4b).

20. *Ned.* 20b, *Eruv.* 100b.

21. *Ned.* 20b.

22. *Pes.* 49b.

23. *Iggeret ha-Kodesh,* quoted in *Kitvei ha-Ramban,* ed. Chavel, 2: 336.

24. *Sotah* 47a.

25. Raavad, *Baal ha-Nefesh* p. 123.

26. *Nid.* 71a, 31b in Rashi; *Eruv.* 100b; *Ḥag.* 5b.

27. This point is not completely clear; see Maimonides, *Ishut* 15:18. But see Rashi, *Shab.* 140b, for possible exceptions.

28. *Eruv.* 100b.

29. See Rashi to *Shab.* 140b D"H *Marginitah Aḥvin Ley* for a variation of this.

30. Maimonides, *Hil. Ishut* 15:17–18.

31. David H. Feldman, *Birth Control in Jewish Law* (New York: New York University Press, 1968), p. 64, makes this point very clearly. He quotes from *McCall's* (November 1966), where W. H. Masters and V. E. Johnson write: "The concept bolstered by ancient laws that sex is a husband's right and a wife's duty has made and continues to make for marriages in which sexuality is exploited and dishonored" (p. 173).

32. *Ket.* 36a; Maimonides, *Hil. Ishut* 12:7; *S. A. Even ha-Ezer 38:5.*

33. *B.M.* 51a, *B.B.* 126b, *Ket.* 61b.

34. One of the implicit assumptions of the entire theory of marital relations is that the quality of the relationship determines the quality of the offspring. See *Ned.* 20b and *Iggeret ha-Kodesh* throughout.

35. *Ḥinukh,* commandment 582.

36. Feldman, *Birth Control in Jewish Law,* makes this point and contrasts it with the Christian view.

37. Maimonides, *Sefer ha-Mitzvot,* negative commandment 355; *Ishut* 1:4; *Melakhim* 4:4.

38. Naḥmanides, *Comments to Sefer ha-Mitzvot, shoresh ḥamishi.*

39. *Magid Mishnah* to *Ishut* 1:4.

40. *Beur ha-Grah* to *Sh. A. Even ha-Ezer* 26:8.

41. *A.Z.* 36b.

Chapter 19

1. Raavad, *Baal ha-Nefesh* (Jerusalem: Mosad Harav Kook, 1964), p. 15.

2. Maimonides, *Hil. Issurei Biah,* chap. 11. Many excellent handbooks on the subject of family purity have been published in the past few years. R. Abraham Blumenkrantz, *The Laws of Nidah: A Digest,* and R. Kalman Kahane, *Daughter of Israel,* are the most detailed halakhic works in English. R. Moses David Tendler, *Pardes Rimonim,* combines medical and halakhic viewpoints. R. Norman Lamm, *A Hedge of Roses,* presents the laws in the perspective of the Jewish approach to marriage, family, and sexuality. R. Zev Schostak, *A Guide to the Understanding and Observance of the Jewish Family Laws,* combines all three approaches.

3. At this point it would be wise to reiterate the simple fact that there is a difference between a post facto investigation of the consequences of life under the mitzvot and the reason for the mitzvot. This discussion is oriented to the first question, not the second.

4. The following examples are not meant to provide a Jewish view of sexuality, but only the responses communicated to me by various individuals.

5. *Nid.* 31b.

6. I would like to thank Linda and Dale Gottlieb for many of the above insights.

7. See in this context R. Norman Lamm, *A Hedge of Roses* (New York: Feldheim, 1972), p. 63

8. *Israel Magazine* 4, no. 2 (February 1972).

9. R. Moshe Tendler, *Pardes Rimonim: A Marriage Manual for the Jewish Family,* p. 13; M. Coppleson, in *British Journal of Hospital Medicine,* 1969, pp. 961–80; A. Singer et al., editorial in *Medical Journal of Australia,* 1968, p. 1138.

Chapter 20

1. See *Ta'an.* 2a; Maimonides, *Tefillah* 1:1.

2. See *Ber.* 31a.

3. *Suk.* 38b.

4. *Ber.* 3:3.

5. The straightforward interpretation of the Yerushalmi is: "It is logical that each man should ask for mercy by himself." See Meiri to *R.H.* 29a, and see *Shaarei Simḥa* of R. Yitzhak Gaius in the section on *Rosh HaShannah,* who says that the same principle underlies silence during prayer and the impossibility of proxy for prayer.

6. *Ber.* 20b.

7. *Ber.* 20a, b.

8. Ibid.

9. Rif to *Ber.* 20b.

10. Maimonides, *Hil. Tefillah* 1:1–3.

11. Ibid.

12. Support for this is found in Maimonides' *Commentary to the Mishnah*, where he says: "The eating of matzah, rejoicing on the holidays, *hakhel*, prayer, reading the Megillah, lighting the Ḥannukah candles, lighting the Sabbath candles, and Kiddush are all time-bound positive commandments, and in each of them the obligation of women is identical to that of men" (*Commentary to Kiddushin* 1:7). If the statement that prayer is a time-bound positive commandment in which men and women are identically obligated is interpreted as referring to the rabbinic obligation, then Maimonides' statement would agree with Rashi and Tosafot and be in consonance with his previously stated position.

13. *Pri Megadim*, general introduction to the Laws of Prayer.

14. Meiri to *Ber.* 20b; *Shaagat Aryeh*, sec. 14; *Arukh ha-Shulḥan, Oraḥ Ḥayim* 106:5; *Megilat Esther* to positive commandment 5; *Ainayim la-Mishpat* to *Ber.* 20b.

15. *Magen Avraham* to *Oraḥ Ḥayim* 106:2

16. This is implicit in his comments to *Oraḥ Ḥayim* 70:1, 299:10. This fact was noticed by *Pri Ḥodosh, Pri Megadim, Mishnah Berurah*, and *Magen Gibborim*.

17. *Mishnah Berurah, Magen Gibborim*, and *Eliyahuh Rabbah* to *Oraḥ Ḥayim* 106.

18. *Pri Ḥodosh* to *Oraḥ Ḥayim* 89:1; *Shaagat Aryeh*, sec. 14; *Mishnah Berurah* to *Oraḥ Ḥayim* 106:1.

19. See *Ber.* 27b.

20. See Rosh to *Ber.* 4:7; Maimonides, *Hil. Tefillah* 1:6.

21. *Mishnah Berurah* to *Oraḥ Ḥayim* 106:1; *Magen Avraham* to *Oraḥ Ḥayim* 299:10.

22. *Oraḥ Ḥayim* 70:1.

23. This view of *ḥazarat ha-shatz* is almost universal. It is a direct implication of many passages in the Talmud, e.g., *R. H.* 34b. It is explicitly stated as above in Maimonides, *Tefillah* 8:1, 8:4, and passim through the rest of chap. 8.

24. Maimonides, *Hil. Tefillah* 8:1.

25. This was overlooked by the Rabbinical Assembly, the rabbinic arm of the Conservative movement, in their decision to include women in the minyan. See Letter to Members of Oct. 5, 1973, esp. the paper of Philip Sigal,

where it is uncritically assumed that communal prayer is an individual obligation.

26. *Pes.* 46a and *Ḥu.* 122b.

27. *Milḥamot ha-Shem* to *Meg.* 5a.

28. *Meg.* 5a.

29. The textual basis for this will be discussed presently.

30. See *R. H.* 29a.

31. *Oraḥ Ḥayim* 55:1.

32. *Ber.* 45b. There is some doubt as to the proper framework for this. Some authorities maintain that it is obligatory on the basis of *Erkhin* 3a. Others maintain that it is optional.

33. Ibid.

34. See Maimonides, *Berakhot* 5:7. *Shiltei Gibborim* in *Berakhot,* chap. 7, says that this view is held by the overwhelming majority of scholars.

35. *Oraḥ Ḥayim* 199:6.

36. See *Shiltei Gibborim* above, for example. Meiri to *Ber.* 47b quotes the opinion and disagrees with it.

37. See *Meg.* 23b.

38. Ibid.

39. See Rashi, *Ket.* 7b; *Meiri* to *Ber.* 47b.

40. See Meiri, *Ber.* 47b and *Beur ha-Grah* to *Oraḥ Ḥayim* 55:1.

41. See *Mordechai* to *Ber.* 47b.

42. For instance, see David Feldman, "Woman's Role and Jewish Law," *Conservative Judaism* 26, no. 4 (Summer 1972): 35–36; Saul Berman "The Status of Women in Halakhic Judaism," *Tradition* 14, no. 2 (Fall 1973).

43. Feldman, "Woman's Role and Jewish Law." The earliest source known to me for this idea is R. Reuven Margolis, *Margoliot HaYam* (Jerusalem: Mosad Ha Rav Kook, 1958), *Sanhedrin* 74.

44. Ran to *Megillah,* end of chap. 1.

45. The details of these laws vary from authority to authority. I have chosen Maimonides' view as an example. See Maimonides, *Hil. Yesodei ha-Torah,* chap. 5.

46. *Sanh.* 74.

47. Ran to *Meg.* 5a.

48. *Gilyonei ha-Shas* to *Sanh.* 74b.

49. *Meg.* 23b.

50. *Oraḥ Ḥayim* 282:6.

51. Chap. 18, sec. 4.

52. *Meg.* 23a.

53. See *R. H.* 33a in all commentaries; Meiri to *Meg.* 23a.

54. Meiri, loc. cit.

55. Ibid.

56. Maimonides, *Tefillah* 5:5.

57. It is instructive to point out Maslow's observation that feelings of self-consciousness disappear during periods of absorption in a peak-experience. This idea is found throughout Maslow's writings. For instance, see the quotation from the paper he presented in 1961 to the Western Behavioral Science Institute, La Jolla, California, in Colin Wilson, *New Pathways in Psychology* (London: Victor Gollancz, 1972), p. 16.

58. This is, of course, an entire subject in its own right and has to be dealt with in an extensive fashion. See *Yalkut Shimoni* to Deut. 23:15 for a little-known source. The major source material is contained in *Sanctity of the Synagogue*, ed. Baruch Litvin (New York: Spero Foundation, 1959).

59. See *Responsa, Rulings and Customs of Rabbi Meir ben Baruch of Rothenburg*, ed. Cahana (Jerusalem, 1957), ruling 104. His view is quoted by *Hagahot Maimoniyot* to *Tefillah* 12:60. His view is also quoted by *Bais Yosef* to *Oraḥ Ḥayim* 135. In addition, *Beur ha-Grah* to *Oraḥ Ḥayim* 282:3 quotes J.T., *Meg.* 4:3 and *Ket.* 2:11 in support of this view.

60. See the Rama to *Oraḥ Ḥayim* 282:3. *Arukh ha-Shulḥan*, ad loc. says that Rama interprets the Yerushalmi differently than *Beur ha-Grah*.

61. See above, chap. 7.

62. *Meg.* 23a.

63. See. Tos. to *R.H.* 33a, D''H *Hah*.

64. My revered teacher, Rabbi Joseph B. Soloveichik, has told me that he is opposed to such aliyot and has never told any rabbi that they are permitted.

65. The technical permissibility of this practice is also open to much question, for many reasons. See, for instance, *Ber.* 11b.

66. *Hagahot Maimoniyot* to *Talmud Torah* 5:6.

67. *Beit Yoseph* to *Tur, Yoreh Deah* 242.

68. *Sh. A. Yoreh Deah* 242:10.

69. *Ber.* 63a.

Chapter21

1. *Eruv.* 96a.

2. It is unclear whether the primary source is the *Pesikta* or the Yerushalmi. *Magen David*, commentary to the *Pesikta*, ad loc. and *Mareh Panim*, commentary to the Yerushalmi, ad loc., feel that the Yerushalmi is the primary source.

3. *Pesikta Rabbati*, ed. M. Friedmann (Meir Ish Shalom) (Vienna, 1880), sec. 22, p. 112b.

4. J.T., *Ber.* 2:3.

5. The exemption of women from tefillin is deduced in this manner. The example of tefillin is then used by the Talmud in *Kidushin* as the source of women's exemption from all time-bound positive commandments.

6. This phrase does not exist in the text of the Vilna Gaon. The emendation places the story of Mikhal as a subsequent statement to the initial statement and not as a question to it.

7. *Ḥidushei ha-Ramban* to *Kid.* 31a says that both sides disapproved. The difference of opinion in the Yerushalmi concerns whether or not the sages protested. There is no controversy over whether or not they disapproved.

8. Raavad's Commentary to *Torat Kohanim, Dibburah Dinedavah,* chap. 2. The interpretation offered by the Raavad is accepted with slight variation by Tos. to *Eruv.* 96a, *Hidushei ha-Ramban,* and Ritva to *Kid.* 31a, and by R. Meir of Rothenburg. Subsequent to R. Meir of Rothenburg, this view was accepted by virtually all authorities. See also in this regard the *Magen Avraham* to *Orah Hayim* 38:3.

9. One of the garments of the high priest—a band of gold worn on the forehead upon which was inscribed "Sanctified for God." The Talmud in *Yomah* 7b deduces from the verse in Exod. 28:38 that the high preist must always be conscious of the fact that the *tzitz* was on his forehead.

10. These few laws are exemplary, not exhaustive.

11. Maimonides, *Hil. Tefillin* 4:14, 15, 25.

12. See, for instance, *Arukh ha-Shulḥan* to *Oraḥ Ḥayim* 38:6; see also *Responsa of Radvaz,* no. 1151 (vol. 4, no. 80).

13. *Shab.* 49a.

14. See *J.T. Ber.* 2:3, which says that anyone who cannot maintain the standards of Elisha Baal Kenafaim cannot wear tefillin.

15. See above, chap. 10.

16. See *Beth Hillel* to *Yoreh Deah* 182:1; *Petaḥ ha-Devir* to *Oraḥ Ḥayim* 38:2; *Kerem Shlomoh* to *Yoreh Deah* 182; *Derash Avrohom,* vol. 2, p. 138b; *Sdei Ḥemed,* vol. 4, p. 90; *Kaf ha-Ḥayim* to *Oraḥ Ḥayim* 38:2; *Responsa of Maharam Schick* to *Yoreh Deah,* no. 173. *Levush* to *Oraḥ Ḥayim* 17:2; *Artzot ha-Ḥayim* to *Oraḥ Ḥayim* 17:2.

17. *Targum Yonatan ben Uziel* to above.

18. For instance, Onkelos uses this prohibition to forbid women from a combat role in the army (see Onkelos to Deut. 22:5). The Talmud in *Nazir* 58b forbids a man from shaving his armpits and genital areas for cosmetic reasons as a result of the above prohibition. Maimonides limits the prohibition to those locales where this is done only by women. Similarly, there is a discussion (see *Yoreh Deah* 182) about the permissibility of the dyeing of hair by men.

19. *Birkei Yosef* to *Orah Hayim* 38.

20. Rashi to *Eruv.* 96a and *R. H.* 33a.

21. *Orḥot Ḥayim* of R. Aaron ha-Kohen of Lunel, sec. on tefillin, no. 3.

22. *R. H.* 33a, Tos D"H *Hah.*

23. *Responsa, Rulings and Customs of R. Meir ben Barukh of Rothenburg,* ed. Cahana, vol. 1, ruling 34, p. 143.

24. *Tashbaẓ,* sec. 270.

25. *Kol Bo,* sec. 21, Laws of Tefillin, p. 13b.

26. *Beit Yosef* to *Oraḥ Ḥayim* 38.

27. *Beur ha-Grah* to *Oraḥ Ḥayim* 38:2 and most other commentaries assume that R. Yosef Karo adopts the *Kol Bo's* opinion.

28. *Yam Shel Shlomoh, Kidushin,* chap. 1, sec. 64.

29. *Avot* 1:2.

Chapter 22

1. See Maimonides, *Tzitzit* 3:1, 10.

2. Ibid., 3:10, 11.

3. Ibid., 3:10.

4. *Yoharah* could alternatively been rendered as "exhibitionism." The exact interpretation is dependent on the issue of whether there is an issue of *yoharah* in the things one does in private. All agree as to the prohibition of *yoharah* on the activities done in public or done in private which become public knowledge. There is some doubt as to its applicability to completely private acts (see *Sdei Ḥemed,* 3:141, Israeli ed.).

5. *Oraḥ Ḥayim* 17:2.

6. *Ber.* 16b.

7. *Ber.* 17b.

8. *Oraḥ Ḥayim* 34:3.

9. Rashi and Rabbenu Tam disagree on the proper manner of preparing tefillin. Most people wear tefillin which accord with the opinion of Rashi. Some people put on a second pair of tefillin at the end of the service, to accord with the opinion of Rabbenu Tam.

Chapter 23

1. Maimonides, *Guide to the Perplexed,* p. 3, chaps. 29, 37; Zev Yavetz, *Sefer Toldot Yisrael,* 10:205.

2. See *Igrot ha-Rambam,* ed. Kapach (Jerusalem, 1972), p. 23.

3. For a detailed treatment of the structure of the oral law, see Harry C. Schimmel, *The Oral Law,* (Jerusalem: Feldheim, 1973).

4. See, in this context, A. H. Maslow, *Farther Reaches of Human Experience* (New York: Viking Press, 1971), p. 45.

5. See *Otzar ha-Geonim* to *Shabbat,* 160–61.

6. *Shab.* 156a.

7. *Eduy.* 5:6.

8. *Oraḥ Ḥayim* 1:1 in Rama.

9. *Yeb.* 62b. See Maimonides, *Hil. Ishut* 15:19.

10. See *ARN* 11:1 passim in the standard version.

11. This is not contradicted by Judaism's praise of the learning of Torah as man's highest activity. See above, chap. 6.

12. See, for instance, Betty Friedan, *The Feminine Mystique* (New York, 1963), p. 41 and throughout.

13. Many of the ideas in this paragraph were inspired by Philip Slater, *Pursuit of Loneliness* (Boston: Beacon Press, 1971).

14. Harvey Cox, *The Secular City* (New York: Macmillan Co., 1969).

15. Jessie Bernard, "The Paradox of the Happy Housewife," in *51 Per Cent* ed. Vivian Gornick and Barbara Moran (New York: Basic Books, 1971).

16. See, for instance, Friedan, *Feminine Mystique,* pp. 40–41.

17. See *Avot* 6:2. Technically, this is not part of the Talmud, but an independent Baraitah.

18. Song of Songs R. 7:3.

19. See *Ta'an.* 2b.

20. See *Shab.* 31a.

Bibliography

The list that follows is, in effect, a bibliographical index. The works are classified in groupings appropriate to their character. Within each grouping, major works are followed by their commentaries, listed chronologically. Explanatory comments are added to facilitate research work for the reader unfamiliar with Hebrew bibliography.

BIBLIOGRAPHICAL INDEX OF HEBREW WORKS

Biblical Commentaries

Rashi (R. Shlomoh Yiẓḥaki), 1040–1105.

R. Abraham Ibn Ezra, 1092–1167.

Naḥmanides (Ramban, R. Moses ben Naḥman), ca. 1195–1270.

The above three are the basic early medieval commentaries to the Pentateuch.

R. Baḥya ben Asher, d. 1340, *Midrash Rabbenue Baḥya al ha-Torah.*

Vilna Gaon (R. Elijah, Gaon of Vilna), 1720–1797, *Aderet Eliyahu.*

Azulay, R. Ḥayim Yosef David (Ḥidah), 1724–1806, *P'nei David.*

Hirsch, R. Samson Raphael, 1808–1888, *Commentary to Pentateuch,* (New York, 1971).

———, *Commentary to Psalms* (New York, 1966).

Berlin, R. Naftali Ẓvi Yehudah, (Netziv), 1817–1893, *Ha-amek Davar.*

———, *Commentary to Song of Songs.*

R. Meir Simḥah ha-Kohen, 1845–1926, *Meshekh Ḥokhmah.*

Epstein, R. Barukh ha-Levi, 1860–1942, *Torah Temimah.*

Targum, Midrashim

Targum of Onkelos, 2nd cent. C.E.,The standard Aramaic translation of the Bible.

Targum of Yonatan ben Uziel.
Mekhilta.
Torat Kohanim.
Raavad (R. Abraham ben David), 1125–1198, *Commentary of Raavad.*
Sifre.
Midrash Rabbah.
R. Issahar ben Naftali ha-Kohen, 16th cent., *Matnot Kehunah.*
Midrash Tanḥuma.
Midrash Zutah to Ruth, ed. S. Buber (Berlin, 1894).
Pesiktah Rabbati, ed. M. Friedmann (Meir Ish Shalom) (Vienna, 1880).
Magen David.
Yalkut Shimoni.

Talmud, Text and Commentaries

Mishnah (found in all editions of the Talmud).
Maimonides, Rabbi Moses (Rambam, R. Moshe ben Maimon) 1135–1204, *Commentary to the Mishnah.*
Tosefta (found in many editions of the Talmud).
Talmud (the Babylonian Talmud).
Geonim. Talmudic commentators prior to the 11th century. Many of their writings are collected in *Otzar ha-Geonim,* ed. Benjamin Mannasseh Lewin 1879–1944.
Rabbenu Gershom, 960–1040, *Commentary to Baba Batra.*
Rishonim: Talmudic commentators of the 11th through the 15th century.
Rabbenu Ḥananel, 11th cent. His commentary is printed in all standard versions of the Talmud.
Rashi (see above). His commentary is printed in all standard versions of the Talmud.
Tosafot. Analyses of talmudic topics by medieval French and German scholars. They are printed on the standard page of the Talmud. Rabbenu Tam, grandson of Rashi, was a leading scholar in this group.
R. Yitzḥak Gaius (R. Yitzḥak ben Yehudah ibn Ghayyat), ca. 1038–1089, *Shaarei Simḥah.*

Ravyah (R. Eliezer ben Yoel ha-Levi), ca. 1160–ca. 1235, *Sefer Ravyah.*
Naḥmanides (see above), *Ḥiddushei ha-Ramban.*
Rashba (R. Shlomoh ben Abraham ibn Aderet), d. 1310, *Ḥiddushei ha-Rashba.*
R. Yiẓḥak of Korbeil, 13th cent., *Sefer Mitzvot Katan.*
R. Mordechai ben Hillel, d. 1298, *Sefer Mordechai.*
R. Meir Abulafia, ca. 1180–1244, *Yad Ramah* to *Sanhedrin.*
R. Menaḥem ha-Meiri, 1249–1306, *Beit ha-Beḥirah.*
R. Asher ben Yeḥiel (Rosh), ca. 1250–1328, *Commentary and Code to the Talmud.*
Ritva (R. Yom Tov ben Abraham Ishbili), 1270–1340, *Ḥiddushei ha-Ritva.*
RaN (Rabbenu Nissim Gerondi), fl. 1340–1380, *Ḥiddushei ha-RaN.*

Aḥaronim. Talmudic commentators subsequent to the 15th century.
R. Shlomoh Luria, 1510–1573, *Yam Shel Shlomoh.*
R. Hayim Yosef David Azulay (Ḥidah), 1724–1806, *Marit ha-Ayin.*
R. Yosef Engel, 1859–1919, *Gilyonei ha-Shas.*
R. Reuven Margulies, d. 1971, *Margoliot ha-Yam* (Jerusalem: Mosad ha-Rav Kook, 1958).
R. Yitzḥak Arieli, d. 1974, *Ainayim le-Mishpat* to *Berakhot,* (Jerusalem, 1970).

Palestinian Talmud (Jerusalem Talmud, Talmud Yerushalmi)
R. David Fraenkel, 18th cent., *Korban ha-Edah,* printed in all standard versions of the Yerushalmi.

Massekhet Soferim.
Avot De'Rabbi Nathan.

Codes and Commentaries

Geonim
R. Aḥai Gaon, 7th or 8th cent., *Sheiltot.*
Rishonim
R. Yizḥak Alfasi (Rif), 1013–1103, A code composed as a digest of

talmudic discussions. It is found in many editions of the Talmud.

Raavad (see above), *Hasagot ha-Raavad al ha-Rif.*

Naḥmanides (see above), *Milḥamot ha-Shem.*

RaN (see above).

Boaz, Joshua (d. 1557), *Shiltei Gibborim.*

The above commentaries are all printed alongside the Rif's code.

Raavad (See above), *Baal ha-Nefesh.*

Maimonides (see above), *Sefer ha-Mizvot.*

Naḥmanides (see above), *Hasagot ha-Ramban.*

R. Yiẓḥak Leon ben Ẓur (16th cent.), *Megillat Esther.*

———, *Mishnah Torah* or *Yad Ḥazakah*

Raavad (see above), *Hasagot ha-Raavad.*

R. Meir ha-Kohen (13th cent.), *Hagahot Maimoniyot.*

R. Yosef Karo, 1488–1575, *Kesef Mishnah.*

Etiah, R. Yiẓḥak, *Mesharet Moshe,* (Liurno, 1828).

Naḥmanides (see above), *Kitvei ha-Ramban,* ed. Rabbi Charles Chavel (Jerusalem: Mosad ha-Rav Kook, 1964).

R. Aaron ha-Kohen of Lunel (early 14th cent.), *Orḥot Ḥayim.*

R. Aaron ha-Levi of Barcelona (middle 14th cent.), *Sefer ha-Ḥinukh.*

Babad, R. Yosef, ca. 1800–1874, *Minḥat Ḥinukh.*

Kol Bo, author uncertain (14th cent.).

R. Yaakov ben Asher, *Tur.* The *Tur* is composed of four volumes: *Oraḥ Ḥayim, Yoreh Deah, Hoshen Mishpat, Even ha-Ezer.*

Karo, R. Yosef (see above), *Beit Yosef.*

Falk, R. Yehoshua, d. 1614, *Derishah* and *Perishah.*

R. David Abudrahm, d. 1345, *Sefer Abudrahm.*

R. Alexander Susslein, d. 1345, *Sefer Agudah.*

Karo, R. Yosef (see above), *Shulḥan Arukh.* This work is a digest of *Beit Yosef,* commentary to the *Tur.* It is likewise divided into the corresponding four volumes.

Rama (R. Moshe Isserles), ca. 1520–1572.

Gumbiner, R. Abraham, 1635–1683, *Magen Avraham.*

R. David ha-Levi, d. 1667, *Turei Zahav* (*TaZ*).

De Siloh, R. Ḥizkiyah ben David, *Pri Ḥadash* (Amsterdam, 1692).

R. Shmuel ben Uri, d. 1698, *Beit Shmuel.*

Shapiro, R. Eliyahu ben R. Wolf, *Eliyahu Rabbah* (Sulzbach, 1753).
Vilna Gaon (see above), *Beur ha-Grah.*
Azulay, R. Ḥayim Yosef David (Ḥidah), 1724–1806, *Birkei Yosef.*
Teomin, R. Yosef, 1727–1793, *Pri Megadim.*
Ettinger, R. Mordechai Zev, 1804–1863, *Magen Gibborim.*
Malbim, R. Meir Leibush, 1809–1879, *Arẓot ha-Ḥayim.*
Lichtenstein, R. Hillel, 1815–1891, *Beit Hillel.* Standard commentary to *Yoreh Deah,* printed on side of page.
R. Yisroel Meir ha-Kohen (Ḥafeẓ Ḥayim), 1838–1933, *Mishnah Berurah.*
Haas, R. Shlomoh, *Kerem Shlomoh* (Pressburg, 1840).
Pontremoli, R. Ḥayim Binyamin, *Petaḥ ha-Devir* (Izmir, 1855–1873)
Palaggi, R. Yiẓḥak, *Yafeh la-Lev* (Izmir, 1872–1879).
Sofer, R. Yaakov Ḥayim, ca. 1869–1939, *Kaf ha-Ḥayim.*

Jaffe, R. Mordechai, 1530–1612, *Levush.*
R. Shmuel ben R. David ha-Levi, *Naḥlat Shivah* (Amsterdam, 1667). Compilation of laws and documents relating to Jewish family law.
R. Aryeh Leib ben Asher, 1695–1785, *Shaagat Aryeh.*
Danzig, R. Abraham, 1748–1820, *Ḥaye Adam.*
Ashkenazi, R. Nisim Abraham, *Derash Avraham* (Salonica, 1852).
R. Israel Meir ha-Kohen (see above), *Likutei Halakhot.*
Epstein, R. Yeḥiel Michael, 1835–1908, *Arukh ha-Shulḥan.*
Borenstein, R. Abraham, 1839–1910, *Egali Tal.*
Lubetsky, R. Yehudah, *Ain Tnai bi'Nisuin* (Vilna, 1930).
Agudat ha-Rabanim, *Le'Dor Aḥaron* (New York, 1937).
Neumark, R. Abraham, *Eshel Avraham* (Tel Aviv, 1954).
Sorotzkin, R. Zalman, 1881–1966, *Moznaim la-Mishpat* (Jerusalem, 1968).
Katz and Glasner, ed. *Piskei Din shel Batei Din ha-Rabanim be'Yisrael* (Decisions of Israeli Rabbinic Courts).
Berkovits, Dr. Eliezer, *Tnai bi'Nisuin ve'Get* (Jerusalem: Mosad ha-Rav Kook, 1967).

Responsa

R. Meir of Rothenburg, d. 1293, *Responsa of R. Meir of Rothenburg*, ed. Rabinowitz (Lemberg, 1860).
———, *Responsa, Rulings and Customs of Rabbi Meir ben Baruch of Rothenburg*, ed. Cahana (Jerusalem, 1957).
R. Asher ben Yeḥiel (see above), *Teshuvot ha-Rosh*.
Rashba (R. Shlomoh ben Abraham ibn Aderet), d. 1310, *Shaalot U'Teshuvot ha-Rashba ha-Meuḥasot le'ha-Ramban*.
Sofer (Schreiber), A. ed., *Teshuvot Ḥakhmei Provence* [Responsa of the Sages of Provence] (Jerusalem, 1967).
Duran, R. Shimon ben Ẓemaḥ, 1361–1444, *Tashbaẓ*.
Rashbash (son of above), 15th cent., *Teshuvot ha-Rashbash*.
Radvaz (R. David ben Shlomoh ibn abi Zimra), ca. 1479–1589, *Teshuvot ha-Radvaz*.
Rakvalti, R. Shmuel ben R. Elḥanan Yaakov, *Maayan Ganim* (Venice, 1553).
Azulay, R. Ḥayim Yosef David (Ḥidah), 1724–1806, *Tuv Ayin* (Husiatyn, 1904).
Aszod, R. Yehudah, 1794–1866, *Yehudah Yaaleh, Responsa of R. Yehudah Aszod* (Lemberg, 1873).
Schick, R. Moshe, 1805–1879, *Responsa of Maharam Schick*.
Soloveichik, R. Yosef Dov, 1820–1892, *Beth ha-Levi*.
Borenstein, R. Abraham, 1839–1910, *Avnei Nezer*.
Felder, R. Gedaliah, *Yesodei Yeshurun* (Toronto, 1954).

Halakhic Articles and Secondary Sources

Epstein, Louis. *Haẓa'ah Lemaan Takannat Agunot*. (New York, 1930).
———. *Le'Shaalat ha-Agunah*. (New York, 1940).
Freiman, Abraham Ḥayim. *Seder Kiddushin ve'Nisuin* (Jerusalem: Mosad HaRav Kook, 1945).
Zaks, R. Nisan. "Kiddushin al Tnai," *Noam* 1 (1958): 52 ff.
Rabinowitz-Teumim, R. Binyamin. "Self-Imposed Constraint in Divorce," *Noam* 1 (1958).
Kasher, R. Menaḥem M. "Be'Inyan Tnai bi'Nisuin," *Noam* 2 (1968).
Elinson, R. Eliakim. "Siruv la-Tet Get," *Sinai* 69, nos. 3–4 (1971).

Extra-Legal Works

Maimonides (see above). *Guide to the Perplexed* (*Moreh Nevukhim*).
———. *Igrot ha-Rambam*, ed. Kapach. (Jerusalem: Mosad HaRav Kook, 1972).
Recanti, R. Menaḥem ben Binyamin, d. ca. 1290. *Ta'amei ha-Mitzvot*. London, 1962.
Maharal (R. Yehudah Loew ben Beẓalel), d. 1609. *Sifrei Maharal*. Jerusalem, 1971.
R. Shneur Zalman ben Barukh, 1747–1812. *Likkutei Amorim Tanya*.
Hirsch, R. Samson Raphael, 1808–1888. *The Hirsch Siddur* Jerusalem: Feldheim, 1972.
Yavetz, Zev. *Sefer Toldot Yisrael*. Tel-Aviv, 1932.
Soloveitchik, R. Yosef Dov. "Ish ha-Halakhah," *Talpioth*, vol. 1.
———. "Mah Dodekh mi'Dod," *HaDoar*, 42, no. 39 (1963).
Margolyot, R. Asher Yishayahu Zelig. *Daat ha-Kedoshah*. Jerusalem, 1969.

BIBLIOGRAPHY OF ENGLISH WORKS

Adler, Rachel. "The Jew Who Wasn't There: Halakhah and the Jewish Woman." *Davka* (Summer 1971): 6–11.
Angus, S. *Environment of Early Christianity*. New York, 1915.
———. *Religious Quest of the Graeco-Roman World*. New York, 1929.
Appel, Gersion. *A Philosophy of Mitzvot*. New York: KTAV, 3975.
Atkinson, Thomas E. *Wills*. St. Paul, Minn.: West Publishing, 1953.
Berman, Saul. "The Status of Women in Halachic Judaism." *Tradition* 14, no. 2 (Fall 1973).
Bernard, Jessie. "The Paradox of the Happy Housewife." In *51 Per Cent*, edited by Vivian Gornick and Barbara Moran, New York: Basic Books, 1971.
Bigelow. "Theory of Post-Mortem Disposition: Rise of the English Will." 11 *Harvard L.R.* 70.
Blumenkrantz, Rabbi Abraham. *The Laws of Niddah, A Digest*.
Connor, James T. "The Nature of Succession." 8 *Fordham Law Review* 152.
Cox, Harvey. *The Secular City*. New York: Macmillan Co., 1969.

Feldman, David. *Birth Control in Jewish Law.* New York: New York University Press, 1968.

———. "Women's Role and Jewish Law." *Conservative Judaism* 26, no. 4 (Summer 1972).

Friedan, Betty. *The Feminine Mystique.* New York, 1963.

Gittelsohn, Roland B. "Women's Lib and Judaism." *Midstream* 17 (October 1971): 51–58.

Gutstein, Solomon. "Civil Enforceability of Religious Antenuptial Agreements." 23 *University of Chicago Law Review* 122.

Hyman, Paula. "The Other Half: Woman in Jewish Tradition." *Conservative Judaism* (Summer 1972): 14–21.

Interpreter's Bible. New York, 1951–1957.

Kahane, Rabbi Kalman. *Daughter of Israel.* Jerusalem: Feldheim, 1973.

———. *Theory of Marriage in Jewish Law.* Leiden:Brill, 1966.

Kierkegaard, Sören. *The Sickness Unto Death.* New York: Doubleday, 1953.

Lamm, Rabbi Norman. *A Hedge of Roses.* New York: Feldheim, 1972.

———. "Recent Additions to the Ketubah." *Tradition* 2, no. 1 (Fall 1959).

Levin, A. Leo, and Kramer, Meyer. *New Provisions in the Kethubah.* New York: Yeshiva University, 1955.

Litvin, Baruch, ed. *Sanctity of the Synagogue.* New York: Spero Foundation, 1959.

Maslow, A.H. *Farther Reaches of Human Experience.* New York: Viking Press, 1971.

Meiselman, Moshe. "Women and Judaism: A Rejoinder." *Tradition* 3, no. 2 (Fall 1975): 52–68.

Otto, Rudolf. *The Idea of the Holy.* New York: Oxford University Press, 1923.

Philo. *Works.* Translated by F. H. Colson and G. H. Whitaker. Loeb Classical Library. Cambridge: Harvard University Press, 1932.

Schostak, Rabbi Zev. *A Guide to the Understanding and Observance of the Jewish Family Laws.* Jerusalem: Feldheim, 1971.

Slater, Philip. *Pursuit of Loneliness.* Boston: Beacon Press, 1971.

Soloveichik, Rabbi Joseph B. "Lonely Man of Faith." *Tradition* 7, no. 2 (Summer 1965).

———. *Shiurei HaRav: A Conspectus of the Public Lectures of Rabbi Joseph B. Soloveichik*. New York, 1974.

Stolper, Pinchas. *Tzniut: The Road to Responsible Jewish Adulthood*. New York, 1967.

Tendler, Rabbi Moses David. *Pardes Rimonim: A Marriage Manual for the Jewish Family*.

Wilson, Colin. *New Pathways in Psychology*. London: Victor Gollancz, 1972.

Glossary of Hebrew Terms

Words set in SMALL CAPITALS are defined elsewhere in the Glossary

AGUNAH. Lit., a "chained woman." This refers to a woman whose marriage has been terminated de facto but not de jure, and who is, hence, incapable of remarrying because she is still technically married to her previous husband.

AKEDAH. The test of Abraham, where he was required to offer his son Isaac as a sacrifice, recorded in Genesis 19:1–19.

ALIYAH. The recitation of blessings over the TORAH before and after each section of the communal Torah reading.

AM HA-ARETZ. An ignoramus who is not to be trusted on ritual matters.

AMIDAH. The central prayer in the Jewish liturgy. It is recited three times daily—morning, afternoon, and evening. During communal prayer, the ḤAZAN repeats this prayer in the morning and afternoon, after the individual congregants have recited it individually.

AMORA (pl. AMORAIM). A scholar of the talmudic period; i.e., the third through the fifth century of the common era.

ASMAKHTA. An indeterminate contract, invalidated by the HALAKHAH due to its vagueness.

BETH-DIN. A Jewish court empowered by Jewish law to decide and enforce questions of HALAKHAH.

BIRKAT HODO'OH (pl. BIRKOT HODO'OH). Blessings recited out of gratitude.

BIRKAT SHEVAḤ (pl. BIRKOT SHEVAḤ). Blessings recited in praise of God.

BORKHU. A prayer recited during the morning and evening prayers and before the communal Torah reading. The ḤAZAN declares: "Praise the Lord, the source of blessings." The congregation replies: "May the Lord, source of blessings, be praised for ever and ever." This prayer requires a MINYAN.

BRIT-MILAH. The covenant of circumcision, required of all Jewish male children on the eighth day of their lives.

EDAH. A congregation—a group of people who combine as a unit for the purpose of divine service.

EDUT. Testimony.

ESHET ḤAYIL. The proverbial ideal woman as described in Proverbs 31:10–31.

GEONIM. Babylonian scholars from the seventh through the eleventh century.

GET. A Jewish document of divorce which must be handed by the husband to the wife to terminate a Jewish marriage.

GEZERAH SHAVAH. A technique for equating two concepts, for the purpose of legal detail, based upon formal similarity of biblical terminology rather than similarity of concept.

GEZERAT HAKATUV. An arbitrary decree of the written law, with no apparent logical justification.

GEZERAT HAMELEKH. An arbitrary decree of the TORAH with no apparent logical justification.

GOLEM. A lifeless form endowed with life by a mystical process; often used to refer to a robotlike creature.

HAKAFAH (pl. HAKAFOT). The ceremony of marching around the synagogue with TORAH scrolls on SIMḤAT TORAH.

HALAKHAH. The Jewish system of law and way of life.

ḤAMETZ. Leavened grain products, forbidden during the Passover holiday.

ḤANNUKAH. The holiday celebrating the victory over the Syrian Greeks. The major symbol of this eight-day holiday is the kindling of lights every night of the holiday.

ḤAZAN. The leader of public worship. The major role of the *ḥazan* during the morning and afternoon prayers is the repetition of the AMIDAH.

HEDYOT. A common ignoramus.

ḤELEV. A form of animal fat, forbidden to be eaten by Jewish law.

ḤEREM. A rabbinic excommunication.

ḤESED. Loving-kindness; the fundamental character trait of concern for the welfare of others, arising out of a feeling of identification with the problems and concerns of others.

HILKHOT. Laws.

ISSUR ASSEI. A prohibition which arises as a corollary of a positive commandment.

KADDISH. A prayer which contains the highest form of praise of God. It is utilized as an integral portion of communal prayer and is also recited by mourners on behalf of their deceased relatives. It can be recited only in the presence of a MINYAN.

KASHRUT. The system of dietary laws of the HALAKHAH.

KEDUSHAH. A prayer expressing praise of God which centers around verses in Isaiah and Ezekiel. It is inserted in the repetition of the AMIDAH by the ḤAZAN, and is only recited in the presence of a MINYAN.

KETUBAH. The Jewish marriage contract.

KIDDUSH. The prayer recited before the Sabbath meal that explains the significance of the Sabbath.

KINYAN. A formal act whose purpose is to effect a change in status, either financial or ritual.

KINYAN ISSUR. A KINYAN whose purpose is to effect a ritual change.

KINYAN MAMON. A KINYAN whose purpose is to effect a change in financial matters.

KORET HA-BRIT. A blessing recited during the circumcision ceremony.

LEKHOH-DODI. A song which forms part of the Friday night service, composed by Solomon Alkabetz Ha-Levi (ca. 1540 C.E.). It refers to the Sabbath as the bride of the Jewish people.

LULAV. A palm branch taken as part of the ritual on the festival of SUKKOT.

MA'ARIV. The daily evening prayers.

MEḤITZAH. The separation between men and women in the synagogue.

MEGILLAH. The scroll of Esther, read in the synagogue on PURIM.

MEILAH. The crime of using property which has been sanctified and designated for Temple use for one's own private purposes.

MEZUZAH. Scrolls of parchment upon which is written parts of the TORAH, which are placed upon the doorposts of all Jewish homes.

MIKVAH. A ritual bath used for the purposes of ritual purification.

MINYAN. A group of people containing a minimum of ten adult Jewish males; the basic unit of community for purposes of Jewish prayer.

MITZVAH (pl. MITZVOT). A divine commandment whose fulfillment is an essentially meaningful act.

NIDDAH. A menstruating woman.

OMEN. Architect.

OMER. A sacrifice brought on the second day of Passover. There is a commandment to count each day from the second day of Passover until the holiday of SHEVUOT, a total of forty-nine days. This is refered to as the counting of the OMER.

ONAH. The obligation of the husband to maintain regular marital relations with his wife.

PURIM. The holiday celebrating the victory of the Jews over their Persian enemies in the time of Mordecai and Esther.

RISHON (pl. RISHONIM). European scholars of the eleventh through the fifteenth century.

ROSH HASHANAH. The holiday celebrating the beginning of the Jewish year, marked by the blowing of the SHOFAR, a ram's horn.

ROSH ḤODESH. The holiday celebrating the beginning of each Jewish month.

SEDER. The festive celebration on the first and second nights of Passover where the story of the exodus from Egypt is recited.

SHALOM ZAKHOR. The celebration held on the Friday night following the birth of a baby boy.

SHEMA. The ritual recitation of Deuteronomy 6:4–9, 11:13–21, and Numbers 15:37–41 which forms part of the morning and evening service.

SHEMINI ATZERET. The holiday that concludes the autumn holiday season, occurring on the last days of SUKKOT. The last day of Shemini Atzeret is SIMḤAT TORAH.

SHEVUOT. The holiday seven weeks after Passover, celebrating the beginnings of the harvest and the giving of the TORAH.

SHOFAR. A ram's horn. The blowing of the shofar is a central ritual on Rosh HaShannah.

SHUMAN. The type of animal fat permitted by the laws of KASHRUT.

SIMḤAT BAT. A recent form of ritual ceremony celebrating the birth of a daughter.

SIMḤAT TORAH. The last day of SHEMINI ATZERET. It is a day of special rejoicing because the yearly cycle of TORAH reading is completed on that day.

SUKKAH (pl. SUKKOT). A temporary dwelling. One of the central requirements of the autumn holiday of SUKKOT is to dwell in these temporary dwellings during the holiday.

SUKKOT. plural of SUKKAH; the autumn holiday held five days after Yom Kippur.

TAKANNAH (pl. TAKKANOT). Legislation by a duly constituted rabbinic court.

TALLIT. A four-cornered prayer shawl with TZITZIT on its corners.

TEFILLIN. Phylacteries, black leather boxes bound to the arm and head during prayer.

TIFLUT. Alternately translated as "immorality" and "irrelevancies."

TORAH. The entirety of Jewish law and ideology.

TZITZIT. Fringes attached to the corners of all four-cornered garments worn by male Jews.

TZNIUT. Privacy; refers to covering the body and to an inner-directed orientation of one's activities.

YEDIAH. Knowledge; sexual relations between husband and wife.

YOHARAH. False religious pride and exhibitionism.

Index